About the Author

YAYORI MATSUI was for over thirty years a journalist on *Asahi Shimbun*, one of Japan's leading newspapers. Author of many books, including the best-selling *Women's Asia* (Iwanami Shoten, 1987), she is one of the founders of the Asia–Japan Women's Resource Centre, and editor of the journal *Women's 21st Century*.

WOMEN IN THE NEW ASIA
From Pain to Power

Yayori Matsui

Translated by Noriko Toyokawa
& Carolyn Francis

WHITE LOTUS
Bangkok

SPINIFEX PRESS
Victoria

ZED BOOKS
London & New York

Women in the New Asia was first published
as *Onnatachi ga Tsukuro Asia* by Iwanami Shoten, Tokyo, 1996

First published in English by
Zed Books Ltd, 7 Cynthia Street, London N1 9JF, UK,
and Room 400, 175 Fifth Avenue, New York, NY 10010, USA in 1999

Published in Thailand by White Lotus Company Ltd,
GPO Box 1141, Bangkok, 100501

Published in Australia and New Zealand by Spinifex Press,
504 Queensbury Street, North Melbourne, Victoria, 3003, Australia

Distributed in the USA exclusively by St Martin's Press, Inc.,
175 Fifth Avenue, New York, NY 10010, USA

Typeset by Lucy Morton & Robin Gable, Grosmont
Cover designed by Andrew Corbett
Printed and bound in the United Kingdom
by Biddles Ltd, Guildford and King's Lynn

A catalogue record for this book is available from the British Library

ISBN 1 85649 625 2 (Hb)
ISBN 1 85649 626 0 (Pb)

White Lotus ISBN 979 8434 66 4

Spinifex ISBN 1 87555986 8

Contents

Preface to the
English Edition

Approximately ten years have passed since the publication of my earlier book, *Women's Asia*. In that time, Asia has achieved rapid economic development, attracting worldwide attention. It is said that the twenty-first century will be Asia's century. Most economists have glorified the Asian economic miracle.

If it has been such a miracle, why has the number of young Asian women having to migrate to Japan in search of work increased so substantially during the 1990s? This is just one example of the other face of Asian economic growth. After all, it was in the midst of economic growth and prosperity that Asian women suffered most from the feminization of poverty and an increase in violence, as well as from many other violations of human rights and unprecedented environmental destruction in the region. This is why Asian women began to question this type of economic development and to display a remarkable capacity for confronting and overcoming some severe obstacles.

The basic contradictions of Asian economic growth, which women had already experienced, were suddenly revealed in 1997 for all to see and experience. The financial crisis hit Thailand, Indonesia and other Southeast Asian countries, as well as Korea, putting an end to their dream of eternal prosperity. It has been a decade of dramatic change for Asia.

During the same period, my personal life also underwent a significant change. I retired from *Asahi Shimbun* in 1994, completing thirty-three years as a newspaper journalist. While continuing my writing career as a freelance journalist, I founded the Asia–Japan Women's Resource Centre in 1995.

My involvement in Asian issues started a quarter of a century ago, based on my experience as a journalist. Japan was in the midst of an economic boom when I became a reporter for *Asahi Shimbun*, a leading Japanese nationwide newspaper, in 1961. I was the only woman the company hired that year. I was interested mainly in the serious problems caused by the overly rapid economic growth of the 1960s, such as industrial pollution, and I covered the Minamata mercury-poisoning and Itai-itai cadmium-poisoning cases, in which a number of people were killed. It was painful to report on these tragedies, but at the same time I was deeply moved to see that those who suffered most – women in poor, remote villages – fought back most courageously.

Women also took the lead in the nationwide anti-pollution struggles of the early 1970s. Therefore I highlighted the importance of women's intervention in the realm of environmental protection. I also tried to expose problems of food, pesticide, drug and consumer-product safety, issues many newly formed women's groups were tackling. Japanese women played prominent roles in the environmental movement as well as in the peace movement and were in fact the driving force behind these campaigns.

I had a lonely fight in the newspaper company – a man's world – as in those days my male colleagues were rarely interested in environmental issues. Editors were afraid of hurting corporations and only reluctantly agreed to publish my stories. The growing environmental movement forced the government to introduce new pollution-control laws; court cases were won by victims. A typical response of many companies was to relocate their plants to neighbouring Asian countries: this was tantamount to exporting pollution. I tracked down the companies who were fleeing from Japan and in the mid-1970s began to visit the areas surrounding their new plants. I was profoundly shocked; I had never imagined the extent of Japanese economic activity in other Asian countries. The issue of the export of pollution awakened me to the reality of Asia–Japan relations.

Another issue that made me pay attention to the interaction between Japan and the rest of Asia was that of the sex tours taken by Japanese men since the early 1970s. A demonstration at Seoul

Airport by young Korean women opened my eyes to the sexual exploitation of women of poorer countries by men of richer countries. After I began investigating sex tours in Asia, I began to analyse the sex tour as a form of both gender discrimination and North South inequality. As I had anticipated, my articles examining Japanese men's sex tours were often rejected by my editors, and male colleagues even showed hostility toward me for my exposés. I felt isolated in the newspaper company. Many of my articles regarding Asia in general were not published by the newspaper.

I was encouraged, however, by the strong support I received from outside the company, especially from women readers. I decided that I would write about Asia for alternative media, no matter how small in circulation, in addition to writing for the mass media. Thus, in 1977, some friends and I founded the Asian Women's Association and began publication of a newsletter, in which I wrote about the structure of sex tours in Asia. Such information was shared by women in the Asian countries invaded by the Japanese male tourists and contributed to the protests sponsored by women's groups.

I became an *Asahi Shimbun* correspondent based in Singapore, where I worked during the first half of the 1980s. My male colleagues preferred to be posted to Western countries, but I was eager to work in Asia and willingly took my assignment to the Singapore bureau. Incredibly, I was then the only female foreign correspondent from a major Japanese newspaper. I made an effort to report on grassroots movements in Asia, a topic male overseas correspondents hardly covered.

Since returning to Japan in 1985, I have been active both as a journalist and as a feminist in various campaigns concerning the relationship between Japan and other Asian countries. My main areas of concern are those involving Asian women victimized by various forms of gender violence: Thai women sold to Japan; Japanese-Filipino children abandoned by Japanese fathers; "comfort women" abused by Japan's military sexual slavery during World War II. I am now engaged in preparations for a Women's International War Crimes Tribunal on Japan's military sexual slavery as a main event of the "Honor and Justice to Comfort Women!" Global Campaign 2000 to be held in December 2000. This is to help put an end to the twentieth century of violence against women and to usher in a twenty-first century of non-violence and peace.

The Asia–Japan Women's Resource Centre, of which I am director, is trying to stimulate as many Japanese women as possible to broaden their perspectives and to take action to protect the human rights of Asian women. For this purpose, it publishes the quarterly periodical *Women's 21st Century*, holds women's empowerment seminars and organizes women's study tours to Asian countries.

It is vitally important for women to strengthen their global solidarity as women in order to confront the globalization of free market economics, a process forcing people to join the race to the bottom. It is women who are most exploited and most oppressed at the poorer end of the Asian spectrum.

I have been able to maintain my involvement in Asian issues for over twenty years because I have always been encouraged and inspired by Asian women who are living with tremendous vivacity and human power under unimaginably hard conditions. In fact, whenever I travel around Asia, I meet many impressive women who have turned their pain into power and have searched for light in the darkness. In knowing them, I truly sense the joy of life.

This book contains reports of my trips to Asia during the past few years. At times I uttered a prayer as I wrote; at other times I wrote filled with excitement. I only hope that this book will be of some help in sharing the pains and joys of women in Asia with many concerned people inside and outside the region; that it thereby contributes to our mutual efforts to explore our common visions for the future. It is my deepest desire that Asian women join together to create a new Asia, an Asia where women and men, nature and human beings, the South and the North can live together.

Yayori Matsui
May 1998

Introduction

Asian Women Today

The Beijing World Women's Conference: The Power of Asian Women

The Fourth UN World Conference on Women was held in Asia in the fall of 1995. Over 40,000 women assembled, filled with excitement and enthusiasm: "Empowerment for women moving forward toward the twenty-first century." I was really overwhelmed by the power of Asian women, especially women at grassroots level. Compared with the International Women's Year World Conference, held in Mexico City twenty years earlier, at which Asian women held a rather low profile, at the Beijing Conference, the first worldwide women's conference held in Asia, Asian women spoke out and acted so powerfully.

For example, from Cambodia, a country isolated from the international community for a quarter of a century due to war and a genocidal regime, 130 women appeared for the first time on the international stage. They called on the women of the world to show global sisterhood and join the "Weaving the World!" campaign, at the climax of which several hundred metres of ribbon woven by women of the whole world was joined together and draped along the Great Wall of China.

Almost all of the Cambodian women who came to Beijing had suffered greatly under the genocidal regimes, which had murdered family members and friends. As a correspondent for *Asahi Shimbun* based in Singapore, I made my first visit to Cambodia in 1982; everywhere I went, I saw mass graves where human bones were piled up or scattered on the ground, testifying to the extermination

The opening ceremony of the NGO Forum at the Fourth UN World
Conference on Women, held in Beijing on 30 August 1995

of as many as two million people in a country of only seven million.
I encountered numerous mourning ceremonies in villages and was
witness to the tears of widows and orphans wherever I went. Despite
such a predicament, however, Cambodian women assumed the roles
of their lost men and took on the challenge of rebuilding their
devastated nation with their bare hands in the period called "Cambodia Year Zero". When I saw these women in the long skirts of
their traditional dress and their bright Khmer smiles in Beijing, I
was deeply moved, thinking of the long journey they had survived,
overcoming deep sorrow, turning their pain into power.

Women of Cambodia and other countries drape handwoven cloth
along the Great Wall of China

Over six hundred Korean women came to Beijing, the largest
number of Korean women ever to attend an international conference.
Koreans also had suffered the violence of a dictatorship for a long
period of time. Countless Korean women have been in the forefront
of the democratic movement, enduring imprisonment and torture,
as well as the slaughter of their husbands and sons. These women,
attired in their colourful traditional dress of long skirts and short
blouses, pounded on small Korean drums during their street demonstrations at the NGO Forum, held in Huairou, a suburb of Beijing.
Former "comfort women", sexual slaves of the Japanese military
during the Asia–Pacific war, shared their testimony of tears. Their
ingenuity in overcoming the language barrier symbolized the strength
of Korean women, who have surmounted the tragedy of their nation.

Thai women from agricultural and fishing villages also displayed
great power. Some three hundred Thai women, who have risked their
lives to protest against environmental destruction and confiscation of
land for economic development, had formed a grassroots women's

network in preparation for the Beijing conference. More than twenty women from this network, chosen as delegates to participate in the NGO Forum, cooked Thai food in their hostels. Dressed in dark-blue cotton farmers' clothes, they spoke out at workshops and organized demonstrations, appealing "Stop trafficking in women!", "Stop dam construction!" and so on. Their actions issued a challenge to the stereotypical image of elegant Thai women graciously and submissively greeting others by joining their palms together. These suntanned women, who had never been abroad and could not speak any English, with the assistance of interpretation by NGO women activists with great dignity boldly expressed opinions based on their own personal experiences on issues such as eucalyptus planting.

The power of Asian women, who have resisted and combated various oppressive, destructive, violent forces – including civil wars, dictatorships and economic colonization – exploded into life at the Beijing Conference, leaving an indelible impression on all participants. It is said that "the twenty-first century will belong to Asia", and Beijing was an indication that Asian women will be the ones who will make that prediction come true.

Platform for Action

The Beijing conference included both the official conference in Beijing, attended by representatives of 189 governments, and the NGO Forum, held at around the same time in Huairou, about fifty kilometres from Beijing, close to the Great Wall of China. The most substantive achievement of the governmental conference was the adoption of the "Platform for Action", which begins with the statement, "The Platform for Action is an agenda for women's empowerment." The platform is a guideline for the government of each country, looking toward the twenty-first century.

In order that the platform would reflect their opinions and make the occasion as advantageous as possible to women, NGO women throughout the world started a campaign two or three years before Beijing to debate its content and engage in lobbying activities.

The platform lists twelve critical areas of concern for women and puts forth strategies for the resolution of each one. The twelve areas of concern are poverty, education, health, violence against women, armed conflict, economic participation, decisionmaking, the advancement of women, women's human rights, the media, the environment, and the girl child.

These concerns can be divided into two major categories: the first includes development, economics and North–South issues such as poverty, the environment and economic participation; the second includes such gender issues as violence against women, armed conflict and the girl child. In short, the Platform for Action focus is on development and the human rights of women. What Asian women are confronting is rapid economic development and the accompanying infringement of human rights. During the NGO Forum, women discussed these issues and plans for action in some 4,000 workshops and plenary sessions.

Poverty is the first of the twelve areas of concern in the Platform for Action because, out of the total world population of 5.7 billion, the right of more than 1 billion people to life is threatened by absolute poverty; of that number, between 70 and 80 per cent are women, an indication of the critical issue of the increasing feminization of poverty.

At the Mexico conference in 1975, Mexican President Echeverría stated, "The women who are most discriminated against and oppressed are poverty-stricken mothers who can neither afford to send their children to school, or take them to a doctor when they get sick." When I stepped out of the Mexico City conference hall, filled with the splendid women governmental representatives listening to his speech, I met a barefooted girl selling a handful of gum in the street, an indigenous mother carrying her sick baby and begging in the rain and, at night, young girls with undeveloped breasts waiting for male customers. These scenes of poverty remain fresh in my mind to this day.

The Causes and Structures of Poverty

Since that time, a quarter-century has passed. However, far from the problem of poverty being solved, countless women are still suffering its ravages. At the Beijing conference, finding a solution to this critical problem was emphasized as being the most urgent issue. Although the Asian economy has developed rapidly since the 1980s to the degree that Asia is now viewed as the development centre of the world, the largest number of impoverished women live in Asia.

Thus, the feminization of poverty is still a most urgent issue for Asia. What are the causes of poverty? Who is responsible? In Beijing, women raised questions regarding the global economic system that has impoverished people in the South.

First, the women of the South joined together to criticize the Structural Adjustment Program (SAP) of the World Bank and its affiliated institutions. The majority of the governments of developing countries have borne enormous debts since the 1980s. International financial institutions in creditor countries have forced debtor countries to adjust economic structures in order to repay their debts. Consequently, governments of developing countries are forced to cut social welfare budgets or privatize public enterprises; as a result they lay off female employees. Furthermore, the SAP forces governments of developing countries to adopt agricultural policies that earn foreign currency; this forces farmers to produce cash crops for export rather than foodstuffs for their own sustenance, which results in food shortage.

Consequently, in Beijing women from India and the African countries, one after another, protested directly to the president of the World Bank, saying "Stop SAP! It robs us of our livelihood!" and "Cancel the debts of the most poverty-stricken countries!" Each day, demonstrations and rallies in opposition to the SAP were held at the NGO Forum. Women of the North, aware of the responsibility their own countries bear as creditors – the contingent from Canada, for example – also actively organized a protest against the G-7 countries. I joined this campaign, because I felt that the women of Japan, one of the largest creditor countries in the world, should not shrink from responsibility in this regard.

Official Development Assistance (ODA) was also a target of condemnation by the NGO Forum as a cause of poverty. At the workshop on ODA, conducted by Group 10, an amalgamation of ten women's organizations in the Philippines, speakers presented first-hand reports of cases that showed how local people were displaced from their communities by large-scale development projects funded by ODA, such as the construction of dams, ports and highways. Such development projects even threaten people's lives. The focus of criticism was Japan, the largest ODA donor country in the world.

Overseas investment of big businesses was another area of concern, as transnational corporations (TNCs) have strengthened their economic activities across national borders. Governments of developing countries have welcomed TNCs, extending them tax breaks and other privileges to promote industrialization in an effort to "Catch up with and surpass the North". The overwhelming majority of employees in such TNC factories are young, single women, many of whom are forced to work for low wages, suffer occupational diseases stemming from poor working conditions, perish in factory fires or are exposed to sexual violence including sexual harassment. The common experience of women's labour in many developing countries was revealed in hundreds of workshops at the NGO Forum.

As for trade issues, women at the NGO Forum joined together to criticize trade liberalization that benefits only developed countries, such as the General Agreement on Tariffs and Trade (GATT). In Beijing again and again I heard the cries of Asian women saying, "Our rural communities were destroyed by agricultural products imported from developed countries, such as the USA, made possible by trade liberalization."

Today, unprecedented numbers of people are driven overseas as migrant workers in search of work. Among them, the number of female migrant workers has drastically increased, resulting in the so-called feminization of migration. Young women are being sold into foreign sex industries, for example in Japan. It was pointed out that this is a result of the impoverishment of rural communities, accelerated by the globalization of the free-market economy, which is led by and caters to developed countries.

At the tent of indigenous women at the NGO Forum, women whose lives and cultures are threatened by economic development shared their pain, which they formulated into a strong statement criticizing the violence of economic development.

The Various Forms of Violence against Women

At the NGO Forum, which was held in response to the violation of women's human rights that is an outcome of the economic development of Asia, the most common workshop theme was violence against women. Women from both the North and the South joined together to share their pain and discuss possible actions on issues of common concern: topics ranged from domestic violence by

husbands, rape and sexual harassment, to the traffic in and enslavement of women.

The fourth area of the Platform for Action is violence against
women. "Eliminating trafficking in women" was one of three strategies listed in this area to prevent violence against women, as it has
reached an unprecedented scale in countries of the South, including
the Asian region. Globalization results in a sex industry in which
more and more women are treated as sex objects and sold across
national borders. Thousands of women are sent from Thailand, the
Philippines and other Asian countries to Japan, and today Japan is
known as the largest market for enslaved women in the world.

But we must not overlook the active women's campaigns in most
Asian countries against the traffic in women. For example, women
are waging an all-out battle against this modern form of sexual
slavery and the growing sex industry in Thailand and Nepal.

The fifth area of the Platform for Action, armed conflicts and
women, declares that violence against women in armed conflict
situations should be considered a war crime. It clearly states the
need for full investigation and prosecution of all criminals, and full
redress for women victims, including those of the military sexual
slavery system (the "comfort women" system of the Japanese military). At the NGO Forum, among the many workshops on this topic
was the War Crimes Tribunal, at which Korean and Filipino former
"comfort women" testified to their painful experiences fifty years
ago, as well as to their continued suffering since the end of World
War II, and demanded compensation from the Japanese government. From Japan, women from Okinawa exposed military violence
against women and issued a strong call for the removal of the US
military presence.

An Alternative Vision for the Twenty-first Century

At Beijing, women raised fundamental questions about the system
of development based on a global free-market economy that im-
poverishes women of the South, destroys their environments and
aggravates violence against women. Participants asserted in the Beijing
NGO Declaration, tentatively adopted at the Forum, the need to
change the current development model and create an alternative.

This represents a fundamental criticism of development-oriented Western industrial society, which originated five hundred years ago at the time of Columbus. This criticism is a direct challenge to Western domination based on the colonization of the South, the plunder of the natural environment and the exploitation of women. Women are eagerly anticipating a twenty-first century different from the twentieth, in which they were victims of poverty and violence, and witnessed the birth of an environmental crisis.

As one small step, women are already implementing various alternatives in different parts of Asia. Women engaging in such efforts held workshops to compare their experiences at the NGO Forum. What kind of serious impact does the rapid economic development taking place in Asia have on women? How courageously are they resisting this? What actions are they taking based on new thinking to create an alternative Asia? Seeking the answers to these questions, I set out to travel throughout Asia and visit the places where women are initiating the creation of a new Asia.

Part I

Economic Development and Violence Against Women

Chapter 1

Trafficking in Women

Sold in Japan and Infected with HIV

I was surprised and delighted to see the slim form of Noi (her nickname), a 29-year-old Thai woman, at the opening ceremony of the Fourth UN World Conference on Women held in the Olympic Stadium in Beijing. Noi is the woman who, at the Asian Women's Tribunal held at Chulalongkorn University in Bangkok in December 1994, tearfully testified to her experience of being trafficked to Japan and infected with human immunodeficiency virus (HIV).

The audience fell silent when delicately framed Noi stepped up to the podium following the announcement "You are requested to refrain from taking photographs." She was recruited in her village in northern Thailand with the promise that she would be working in a Thai restaurant in Japan. She accepted the offer because she wanted to be able to purchase farm land and a house for her poverty-stricken parents. When she arrived in Japan, her boss told her, "You have accumulated a debt of 3.5 million yen (US$25,000) and you must pay it back by engaging in prostitution." This money had been paid to the Japanese and Thai agents. In short, Noi was sold for 3.5 million yen. She was not only confined, battered and forced to take customers every day; she was eventually sold twice more. By then her accumulated debts totalled 7 million yen ($50,000), and she discovered that she had become infected with HIV. The third brothel in which she was employed was subsequently raided by the immigration authorities, and she was arrested and deported.

Noi entered a shelter for people infected with HIV, located in a

Women of the world stage a demonstration at the Beijing NGO Forum:
"Stop violence against women"

suburb of Bangkok. There she was interviewed by a freelance Japanese
television journalist. She described her experience in a tearful voice,
saying, "Although I agreed to the interview on condition that my
face and real name be concealed, the TV programme revealed everything. Because of this, I have not been able to return to my home
village. Give me back my honour, my human rights and my justice!"

A scene from the programme, originally broadcast by a Japanese
television company, was projected onto the screen. Noi's lovely face
filled the frame. The faces of the agent and her customers were all
blurred to avoid identification; the name of the brothel was not
revealed. Furthermore, the Japanese reporter suddenly appeared in
Noi's home village without her consent and told her parents what
had happened to their daughter in Japan, although Noi had concealed
the truth from them so that they would not worry. The television
company even broadcast the sight of Noi's mother bursting into
tears of shock at the news. The sound of the sobbing of some three
hundred women participants attending the tribunal from various
Asian countries filled the hall.

The enslavement and exploitation of an impoverished Thai woman as a sexual slave, threatening her life by infecting her with HIV, arresting her as though she were a criminal and bringing disgrace upon her name in the mass media: I could not even look up due to the shock of listening to her speak of Japan's brutal and inhumane infringement of her human rights. As one of the tribunal "judges", I was impressed with her courage in testifying to her experience despite her pain, and I uttered a prayer for her health and long life.

Once again, at the Beijing conference, Noi bared her soul in front of women from all over the world as she testified with great dignity and participated in a Thai women's demonstration. "How many more years can she live?" "I heard that the TV company didn't take the protest lodged by a Japanese women's group seriously." "What does the company think about women's human rights?" asked Noi's supporters, who subsequently issued a strong demand to Japan to accept responsibility for what happened to Noi. Noi is one of tens of thousands of Thai women trafficked to Japan. These "Nois" all share a painful destiny as they live out their tortured existence there.

Committing Murder to Escape from Hell

As soon as I arrived in Japan, I realized that I had been sold. Although I am a human being, my life here was just like that of an animal. I was not allowed to go out, as if my hands and feet were tied. All I knew were the brothel and hotels. Every single day, I had to go out to sleep with men. I was never allowed to take a day off, not even during my menstruation or when I had a high fever. I was forced to go out to serve men. Even if I attempted to escape, I was tracked down by my boss and told that my parents in Thailand would be killed. It is easy to hire professional killers in Thailand.

In September 1991, a case in which three Thai women stabbed a Thai woman boss to death occurred in Shimodate City, Ibaragi Prefecture, about one hundred kilometres northeast of Tokyo. The above statement is part of a letter from defendant "K", who was 25 years old at the time, in which she described the situation that drove her to commit murder.

My family are practising Buddhists, and I have always been taught to be dutiful to my parents. I am the youngest daughter of my parents, who are farmers. We sometimes don't have enough rice to eat. I have witnessed the lifetime of hardship my parents have suffered. When I graduated from the fourth grade of elementary school, I was not able to continue my studies. I worked as a day labourer on farms, in factories and shops, and as a cleaning woman. After I married, however, I was not able to send money home to my parents. When I was considering how I could support my aging parents, I was told that I could send ten to fifteen thousand bahts [around $US300] home to my parents every month if I went to Japan and worked in a restaurant there. I could not earn such a large amount of money even if I worked for a year in Thailand. So I told my parents to open a bank account and let me know the account number so that I could send money to them every month. Then I left for Japan.

However, K's boss in Japan told her, "You have a 3.5 million yen [US$25,000] debt. You must pay me back by working in prostitution." Then her life as a sex slave began. The cost of food and rent was added to her debt. What's more, she was fined 20,000 yen ($150) if she went three days without a customer, and an additional 20,000 yen if she gained one kilogram in weight. Thus, there was no way she could afford to send money home to her parents. She lived a life of daily despair, for if she showed any resistance she was battered by her boss. Another Thai woman in the same bar attempted suicide, hurt by the insulting words that would disgrace her parents. "We want to escape from this hell. But escaping will surely mean the death of our parents. To be free, there is no other alternative except to kill our boss!" The three Thai women carried out their plan.

They escaped, taking the boss's bag, thinking that their passports were in it. They opened the bag to find 7 million yen (US$50,000) in cash, which represented the fees they had earned as prostitutes: 25–35,000 yen per customer. However, the police wrote up the report as a case of murder with intent to rob, due to the Thai defendants' inability to communicate to the Japanese police that they did not kill their boss for money.

"She Bought These Girls"

I observed the court hearing on the Shimodate case. When I looked at the three young women seated in the defendants' seats in front of me, I considered why these women, the likes of whom might be seen in every agricultural area of Thailand, were being judged in the court of a far-off foreign country as criminals guilty of murder and robbery. I reflected that those who should really be on trial were the agents in sex trafficking, who made a huge profit by using innocents who only sought to follow Buddhist teaching and help their poor parents.

The murdered Thai woman boss might have been a former sex slave herself, who clawed her way up from the bottom to the side with the traffickers of sex slaves. The Japanese male owner of the bar appeared in court as a witness, pointing at the three Thai women and testifying, "Because she bought these girls, I assumed that she had disciplined them severely to be obedient." He did not attempt to conceal the fact that he viewed the women as goods to be bought and sold.

The defence lawyers asserted before the Mito District Court, Shimozuma Branch, that "The defendants were victims of human trafficking. What they did was out of necessity, committing murder out of justifiable self-defence." In his final statement, the prosecutor declared, "The defendants came to Japan for the express purpose of engaging in prostitution for the sake of money. They committed murder for the sake of money. To prevent other foreigners from committing crimes, they should receive a heavy sentence!" The prosecution requested that a sentence of life imprisonment be given to the three Thai women. In May 1994, the court delivered its verdict: guilty of murder with intent to rob, just as the prosecutor had claimed. However, the judge stated that "The defendants landed in Japan through illegal human trafficking networks. The pain and humiliation suffered by the defendants are beyond our imagination." To some extent, the judge took into consideration the clear human rights violations revealed in the court case in handing down the sentence of ten years' imprisonment, which was labelled a "charitable sentence" by the mass media.

But the three women appealed the sentence in the Tokyo High Court, declaring, "We are not robbers! We only wanted our freedom, not money!" They made the decision to fight, even though it might result in a delay in their return to Thailand. This represented their ardent desire to be seen as human beings, not as slaves, animals or goods to be bought and sold. In July 1996 the Tokyo High Court amended the sentence to eight years' imprisonment, as a result of the judges' consideration that the first sentence of the district court was too heavy.

The Thai women seated in the defendants' seats occasionally made eye contact and exchanged smiles with the members of their support group, the Group to Support Three Thai Women in the Shimodate Case, sitting in the observers' seats of the courtroom. Although only a small group, the supporters who encouraged these women as they endured the isolation and pain of life in a detention centre in a foreign country for five years represent the conscience of the aggressor country, Japan. Out of this was born a relationship of trust between the three Thai women and their support group that resulted in some 250 letters being written by the three women to share their experiences and thoughts with their supporters. Some of the letters were published in the book *To the Prostitution Society Japan: Letters from Thai Women*.

Japan: The Most Common Destination of the Traffic in Women

One of the reasons that large numbers of Thai women are imported to Japan, the receiving country, is that Japanese society is historically tolerant of prostitution. The other reason is the situation of Thailand, the sending country. Thai women began to be sent to work in the Japanese sex industry in the mid-1980s. The number of enslaved women increased dramatically around 1990. Thai women were sent to Japan on tourist visas or used fake passports, while Filipino women mostly came to Japan legally on entertainers' visas. There are towns nicknamed "Little Bangkok", where hundreds of Thai women live, in Nagano Prefecture and Ibaragi Prefecture. In areas dominated by organized crime (*yakuza*), the women are used as important financial assets. A *yakuza* group that has ten Thai women in its control can gain a billion yen (US$7 million) per year in profits. Thus, *yakuza* confine Thai women and force them to engage in prostitution. If the Thai women resist, they are controlled through violence, threats, rape and drugs.

Three thousand Thai women each year manage to escape from such conditions and make their way to the Thai Embassy in Tokyo. However, other tragic cases in which Thai women, unable to escape, have murdered their overseers have occurred since the Shimodate case. In 1992, six months after the Shimodate case, six Thai women, including a girl only 15 years old, killed their Taiwanese female boss in Shinkoiwa, Katsushika-ku, Tokyo. In September of the same year, five Thai women killed their female boss from Singapore in Mobara city, Chiba Prefecture. Over ten murder cases involving Thai women occurred during that one year, and such cases continue.

Japan has become the most common destination for women who have been sold into sexual slavery, because of the extent of its sex industry, which generates over 4 trillion yen (US$30 billion) annually, a sum equal to the total of Japan's national defence budget, or 1 per cent of the gross national product (GNP). The sex industry compensates for the shortage of young Japanese women by importing Asian women, who are even cheaper to hire.

The reasons for the expansion of the sex industry are twofold: first, the continuing influence in Japanese society of a sexual climate derived from the licensed prostitution system of the feudal era; and second, in today's corporate culture, the existence of a huge number of company warriors who are exhausted by severe competition and in search of comfort.

Poverty in Rural Villages

The economy of Thailand has shown a high rate of growth since the 1980s, almost reaching the level of the newly industrialized economies (NIEs). Bangkok, the capital of Thailand, is crowded with cars; tall buildings line the streets, reflecting prosperity. On the other hand, in rural village areas, farmers are impoverished. The average income of a household in Isan, the most poverty-stricken area in northeast Thailand, is one-tenth of that in Bangkok. Seventy per cent of Isan farmers have incurred debts which they seek to repay by selling their daughters to brothels. Hill-tribe people in northern Thailand, who have been left out of Thai economic development, are driven to escape their extreme poverty by sending their daughters to brothels. Young girls who are thought to be free from HIV/ AIDS are targeted by sex-trafficking agencies.

Japan is deeply involved in the uneven Thai economic development that results in many farmers and hill-tribe people having to sell their daughters. Japanese companies advanced into Thailand from the late 1980s, during the so-called Thai boom. Today, there are

Hill-tribe girls in Thailand: we must protect their future

more than three thousand Japanese companies in Thailand. Japanese factories produce every conceivable product, including chemical food seasoning, wigs and ski gloves. Factories process food, including yakitori (grilled chicken) and dried fish, by taking advantage of low Thai wages, less than one-tenth of wages in Japan. The Thai government promotes tourism, which destroys forests to construct resorts such as golf courses; forces farmers to cultivate vegetable such as onions and corn for Japanese consumption; and fells mangroves along the coastal areas in order to cultivate prawns and shrimp to export to Japan. The Japanese wholesale destruction of Thailand is so great that a song whose words state "Japan eats up forests, fields and beaches of Thailand. Japan roasts all of Thailand" became a hit. A huge amount of official development assistance (ODA) (US$664 million in 1996) from Japan poured into Thailand, most of which was used for the construction of large-scale infrastructure such as highways, harbours, airports, dams, industrial estates and the development of tourism. Little ODA has been spent on agricultural development, education or social welfare.

As the letters written by the Thai women defendants in the Shimodate case indicate, the poverty of farmers is so severe that it is almost unbearable to witness or endure. However, such poverty is not the only reason for trafficking in women. The consumer culture created by Thailand's rapid economic development has even filtered down to remote villages, stimulating people's desire for money. Consequently, some poverty-stricken farmers sacrifice their daughters in order to be able to afford Japanese electronic appliances, motorbikes and agricultural machines.

Burmese and Chinese Girls

After the Thai democratic movement overthrew the military government in 1992, the first civilian government launched a campaign to eliminate child prostitution. Raids on brothels and the extension of compulsory education to include middle school have resulted in a slight decrease in the number of Thai girls sold into prostitution. However, to compensate for the decreased availability of Thai girls, trafficking agencies have come to target young girls in neighbouring countries. This recent trend was revealed at the Conference on Trafficking in Children in Asia, held in Taipei in 1994.

Burmese (Myanmar) girls are prime targets, with some 40,000 being imported into Thailand, according to UNICEF and other organizations' estimates. Some of the girls sent to the northern Thai border are then moved to Bangkok and tourist resorts such as Chiang Mai and Pattaya. The largest number of enslaved Burmese girls are concentrated in Ranon, a fishing port near the southern Thai border, where they are said to be confined in more than forty brothels surrounded by electric fences. The reality of their physical confinement through the use of violence became widely known after a letter seeking help for seventy-three girls reached an NGO in

Bangkok. The 1993 report *A Modern Form of Slavery: Trafficking of Burmese Women and Girls into Brothels in Thailand*, published by the US human rights organization Asia Watch, exposed the modern-day hell and included interviews with victims.

Girls from minority tribal groups in Yungnan Province in the southern part of China are also sent to the northern part of Thailand, and then on to Malaysia and Hong Kong. The Children's Rights Protection Centre in Bangkok, which is involved in rescuing these girls, estimates that there are at least five thousand of them. The report *Chinese Women's Rights: Caught between Tradition and the State*, presented at the NGO Forum of the Beijing women's conference by China Human Rights, a US human rights organization, describes the rampant trafficking in women for sex and marriage in China. The report discloses that some Chinese women are being sold into Thailand and Taiwan.

Representatives attending the Taipei conference on child trafficking from Vietnam and Cambodia reported that the issue of child prostitution has become a serious problem due to the influx of businessmen and foreign tourists, as a result of the transition to a market economy system and the promotion of tourism. This is especially true since Chinese men from Southeast Asian countries such as Thailand, Hong Kong and Taiwan demand young girls, both because of the myth that having sex with a young virgin can restore their youth and because of the fear of HIV.

The number of young Laotian girls sold into Thailand has also been increasing, and instances of the rescue of these girls from brothels near the borders are reported by the mass media. The waves of free-market economics flooding the Asian continent have spread to China, Vietnam, Laos and Cambodia, commercializing everything as a means of profit. Thailand, a leader in economic development in the region, is also exploiting girls in surrounding less-developed countries.

Programmes for the Protection of Girls

Rows of brothels line the streets of Maesai, a town close to the border between northern Thailand and Burma. Not only Thai girls but also girls from hill tribes in Burma are confined here. I found a small daycare centre on the Sai river, which runs between Thailand and Burma. There, in a newly built building, 155 children in dark blue uniforms, ranging in age from 2 to 13 crowd around 22-year-old Janrem Shirikanfu, who seems more like a big sister than a teacher. There are many people from hill-tribes, including Shan and Aka, in her village who have no concept of national borders. Because they do not have Thai nationality and they live in poverty, their children cannot go to school, and 80 per cent of the girls are sold into prostitution.

> Some girls are sent to Bangkok when they are around 7 years old, so I have been thinking about how these girls can stay in the village. I thought that it would make some difference if they could at least read and write. After I graduated from elementary school, I started to teach the children to read and write, using a little financial support from my father.

Janrem was only 14 years old at that time. Several years later, the daycare centre was established with the help of a person who read about her project in a Bangkok newspaper. The building that she had dreamed of was finally completed in 1991, eight years after she began teaching. She works hard alongside three volunteer teachers. She speaks softly but with conviction, "We talk with parents to prevent children from becoming victims of prostitution and drugs, to enable them to live as human beings."

I dropped in at the nearby Daughters' Education Programme. Sompop Jantonaka, a former tour guide, started this project in a borrowed temple at the end of the 1980s. He says, "I saw the inhuman lives of the girls in brothels and wanted to do something to prevent girls from being sold." Showing me a distribution map of the hill tribes, Sompop said, "In this area, even village chiefs, priests, and teachers are involved in sex trafficking. If I get information about a girl who is about to be sold, I convince her parents not to sell her, and we accept the girl here to send her to middle school." More than ten girls dressed in spotless uniforms greeted me shyly upon their return from school. "Girls who had been obedient to their fathers and their elders come here and gain confidence to speak out. This change symbolizes the most positive result of what I am doing." Sompop emphasizes the girls' self-reliance and change in self-awareness. He is committed to challenging not only poverty but also the culture of intense gender discrimination that forces women to become subordinate simply because they are women.

Wanser (third from left) is actively organizing Yao women
at Padeen village in northern Thailand

Forty families of the Yao hill tribe lived in Padeen village close to
the Lao border. More than ten mothers dressed in colourful tribal
clothing sat in a circle at the home of the village head, talking with
a young Yao woman, Wanser Sefun, a 21-year-old member of the
Hill-tribe Women's Education and Development Project, which was
established by a Japanese man. She has lived in this village organizing Yao women for two years, and finally was able to form a
mothers' group. Wanser said, "Hill-tribe people have become poor
as a result of development and deforestation. They suffer from such
problems as trafficking in women and drugs. In order to solve these
problems, women must become aware and take the lead in community development."

One after another, the mothers showed me beautiful embroidered cloth, some of which had letters embroidered on it. Wanser
explained, "This is our programme of literacy education through
embroidery. Women begin by learning how to write their names
and the name of their village. They can also earn income by selling
their handmade products." The mothers began to talk, one after

another. "I have been able to consult with others, even about family matters, such as my relationship with my husband and mother-in-law, since the group was formed." "We can discuss how to prevent our daughters from being sent off to the city." Women who at one stage were not even able to introduce themselves in front of others are now speaking out. Among them was a young mother who shared her tragic experience of being driven to prostitution after she left home due to dissatisfaction regarding the unequal distribution of family land.

Wanser reported on her work at the first Thai Minority Tribal Peoples' Conference, held in Chiang Mai in 1992. The Thai minority number 550,000. Representatives of eleven hill-tribe groups and two maritime tribal groups participated in the conference. In her presentation, Wanser declared that "The minority peoples want to claim the same human rights as Thai people. We women must be granted the same human rights as men." The male elders felt that their traditions were being challenged by this demand for reform. After much heated discussion, the promotion of women's status was clearly stated in the declaration adopted at the Minority Tribal Peoples' Conference. I saw a vision of the future in the struggle of this one young Iao woman.

The Death of a Nepalese Girl

In addition to Thailand and its neighbouring countries, another centre of the traffic in women is South Asia. Especially noticeable here is the large number of Nepalese girls sold into Indian brothels.

When she heard that she would be able to work at a carpet factory in the suburbs of Kathmandu, 15-year-old Maya thought she was dreaming. She believed that she would now be able to escape from the hard labour and starvation in her mountain village in Nuwakott District, northwest of the capital of Nepal. Although the labour at the factory was severe, she was beside herself with joy at being invited to Bombay, "the city of dreams", six months later. She knew that people in the village envied women who returned home "successful" from India.

The carpet factory was only the first step along the road to sexual slavery, and Maya was subsequently sent to Calcutta. She was sold to a brothel in Sonagatte for 25,000 rupees (US$600). Most of the 40,000 trafficked women in this area were Nepalese. Later, Maya was sold for 15,000 rupees ($350) to a Bombay brothel, where she spent two years in sexual slavery. Maya contracted a serious sexually transmitted disease and was hospitalized for three months. She was rescued by a doctor who felt great concern for her, and she returned to the home village she had left with a dream just five years earlier, exhausted both physically and mentally. She died at the very young age of 20 in 1989.

"Approximately 200,000 Nepalese women are being trafficked and are suffering just as Maya did, in the prostitution areas of India." In March 1996, I learned that trafficking in women had emerged as a social problem in Nepal when I visited Kathmandu to participate in the Southern Asia Regional Conference of the People's Plan for the Twenty-first Century (PP-21) on the theme "Searching for the People's Vision for the Twenty-first Century", held just after the Indian government announced that it would deport 218 Nepalese women infected with HIV. Seventeen Nepalese women's NGOs which were addressed on the issue of trafficking appealed directly to the prime minister to develop a policy to care for these women.

I recalled the Nepalese girls I saw in 1983 in Kamatipula (Forkland Avenue), Bombay, one of the largest prostitution areas in the world. I saw many young women lined up in rows in front of the brothels, waiting for customers. Guided by a doctor specializing in sexually transmitted diseases, I visited a brothel; there were more than twenty women working there and all of them were Nepalese. They could do no more than murmur "this is so painful" in front of the owner of the brothel. When I visited their homeland two years later, I learned that approximately 50,000 Nepalese women had been sold throughout India. I was shocked by the fact that, ten years later, the number of women victims had grown to 200,000, and that from 5,000 to 7,000 women are being sold every year.

I visited the Women's Rehabilitation Centre in Kathmandu. The head of the centre is Renu Rajbandri, aged 36, a woman doctor who had been to Japan for medical training:

> Five years ago, I administered an HIV test to a 19-year-old girl who had escaped from a Bombay brothel. That is how it all began. I quit my job at a local health centre and founded an NGO to prevent

trafficking in women. I was so shocked by the girl's tragic experience and her question to me, "What can you do for me as a doctor?", that I made the decision to work against trafficking in women at the grassroots level.

Renu conducted a survey in Bombay in 1993. Studying 500 Nepalese women known as "cage girls" working in brothels, she discovered that most of them were illiterate; 20 per cent were minors, 65–70 per cent were from Mongolian ethnic groups such as Taman and Gurun; and 35–40 per cent had been deceived by their relatives or other people in their villages. These women took between five and thirty-five customers per day, each customer paying 50–200 rupees (between $1 and $5). The women had worked without being paid for the first five to six years, after which they halved their agents' fees. They stayed in Bombay between fifteen and twenty years, and 90 per cent of them did not want to return home. They indicated that if they could return to a normal life, half of them would return home. "The living environment of women in Bombay is deplorable. There is no sanitation, the food they are provided is half-spoiled, they are constantly threatened and exploited by health workers, police and pimps. But they believe that they can neither escape nor do anything to change their situation, and they have even given up raising their voices", Renu declared.

The Prevention of Trafficking through Empowerment

Renu believes that prevention should be given top priority. She stresses the importance of training young women as village leaders in areas where trafficking is rampant, as these women leaders would then be able to take action in villages all over the nation. Renu said, "Trained women leaders can issue warnings in each village and bring girls who are about to be sold to this centre." Several young girls were concentrating on knitting extra-large men's sweaters in one room of the Women's Rehabilitation Centre. Orders from the Netherlands for these sweaters provide the girls with some income. Eleven girls were living together and helping one another to achieve self-reliance.

ABC Nepal was the first organization in Nepal to become involved in the issue of the traffic in women. Durga Gimire, the representative of ABC Nepal, says:

ABC Nepal representative (right) visiting village women near Kathmandu

I founded this organization with friends in 1987, when I realized that
90 per cent of the women of Nepal live in isolated mountain villages,
suffering from poverty and gender discrimination. I felt I had to do
something. When I started a self-support programme for mountain
village women, seeking to address the three areas of agro-forestry,
basic health care and cooperatives, I realized what a critical issue
trafficking in women is.

ABC is also training women for leadership in villages and conducting
campaigns using improvised dramas and songs among illiterate
village people in Sindpalchouk district, a centre of trafficking in
women, and in other places. ABC also sells cassette tapes of original
ABC songs about trafficking in women and HIV prevention. As I
travelled I realized that Nepalese women had been empowered to
engage in such activities as village campaigns and the establishment
of centres in Kathmandu in a way that would have been unimaginable
even ten years ago.

But why is trafficking in women so pervasive and widespread?
Many women's groups are engaged in analysing its causes as well as

urging people to fight against it. The first reason for the traffic in women is poverty. In Nepal, one of the poorest nations in the world, the average annual income per capita is US$180. Second, discrimination against women is a related factor. When baby girls are born, people lament their birth and abuse them. They have no qualms about selling "worthless" daughters. Third, Nepal has a long tradition of prostitution that includes rounding up women to become mistresses in the royal palace and donating daughters to the Hindu temple to become prostitutes. The traffic in women is also a carry-over from the British colonial period: the British military hired Nepalese men as Gurkha soldiers and used Nepalese women in the prostitution area in Bombay. Fourth, there is inadequate legal protection and political attention given to the issue of trafficking. There is a clearly worked-out trafficking route between the prostitution areas in India, the mountain villages and the carpet factories in Nepal. Profits of as much as US$100 can be made from the sale of one girl. Although the reformed civil law related to trafficking agents prescribes a twenty-year prison term, in reality it is not implemented, since some politicians are tied up with trafficking agents. Fifth, we cannot ignore the influence of the globalization of a free-market economic system, which means an influx of foreign capital, the spread of the consumption of the pornographic cultures of the West and Southeast Asia, and the involvement of foreigners in prostitution as a result of the promotion of international tourism.

It is encouraging to see that the Nepalese women's movement has realized that it must not ignore this modern-day system of slavery, but has become actively involved in challenging the fundamental causes of trafficking in women, building a sense of community and conducting education campaigns on women's human rights, self-reliance and empowerment as a means of prevention.

The International Movement to Eliminate Trafficking in Women

Many workshops on the theme of the traffic in women, which is growing with unprecedented speed due to the globalization of the market economy, took place at the NGO Forum of the Beijing women's conference. These workshops emphasized the horrors of trafficking in Asia, which is centred in Thailand and India. They stressed the necessity of strengthening networks in order to achieve a solution to trafficking.

Most important was the realization by the international community that trafficking represents violence against women. In 1993, the UN World Conference on Human Rights, which took place in Vienna, spelled out the concept of women's human rights and pointed to the elimination of trafficking in women as one of the subjects to be addressed in solving the problem of violence against women. The General Assembly of the United Nations also adopted the Declaration on the Elimination of Violence against Women at the end of the same year, categorizing trafficking in women as violence in society.

The Platform for Action, adopted by the Beijing conference, points to violence against women as one of the twelve areas of concern. One of three main strategies to be adopted by the governmental and international organizations to combat violence against women was a set of measures to eliminate trafficking in women, which includes: (1) punishment of perpetrators through both criminal and civil laws; (2) dismantling networks in trafficking; (3) cooperation with NGOs in providing social, medical and psychological care for victims; and (4) educational campaigns to prevent sex tourism and trafficking. This represents great progress from the Nairobi Forward-Looking Strategies for the Advancement of Women toward 2000, which only addressed trafficking in women in a few sentences. This is an indication of how much the situation has deteriorated during the past decade and, consequently, how much women's concerns about trafficking have grown and anti-trafficking activities increased.

Nevertheless, the rapid economic development based on the free-market system in Asia has resulted in the international trafficking of millions of women and children: in short, a system of modern slavery. Therefore, women who are fighting against the traffic in women in various countries keenly realize that this issue cannot be solved without changing the model of development that involves violence against women, the violation of women's human rights and discrimination against women.

Chapter 2

AIDS Attacks Women

A Village in Northern Thailand

"Recently, Buddhist monks in northern Thailand have become very busy. The price of flowers is increasing because of the funerals for people who have died of AIDS in the villages. HIV infection has spread even to housewives. At one hospital, one in three pregnant women is HIV-positive", stated Professor Virada Somswasdi, director of the Women's Studies Centre, Chiang Mai University, at the Seminar on Trafficking in Thai Women held in Tokyo in March 1996.

Concerned about the spread of HIV infection from Europe, North America and Africa to Asia, and from men to women, I travelled throughout Thailand gathering information for a three-part series, "AIDS, Asia, and Women" for *Asahi Shimbun* (17–19 October 1991). I recalled the shock I experienced at the time as I became aware that the victims of the massive increase in the incidence of HIV infection are mostly poverty-stricken women. I saw the anxiety and agony of those who were infected with HIV; at the same time, I was moved by their forward-looking attitudes and the strong desire to continue living as long as possible.

The first three people I met in Thailand who were infected with HIV were AIDS education staff at the Population Development Association (PDA), a family planning organization in Bangkok. PDA is an NGO founded by former minister Mechai Vilabidya, who is known as Mr Condom. He was the leader of the HIV/AIDS prevention campaign at that time. PDA is promoting the prevention of HIV infection; a part of the education project of this campaign entails people with HIV sharing their experiences.

Breecha, 37 years old, who used to work for a bank in Chiang Mai, is the only man among the three HIV-positive educators.

> I went to a brothel just once under the influence of alcohol, and there became infected with HIV. After that, the bank fired me. Losing hope, I contemplated suicide, but I did not do it because my mother cheered me up, telling me that I was her precious son no matter what disease I had. AIDS will not be eradicated unless we eradicate prostitution.

Breecha travels around to many villages to lecture on his experience. He also makes television appearances in which he stresses the importance of prevention.

Tiny Phai, aged 15, was a newlywed wife when she was infected by her husband. Listening to Breecha with tears in her eyes, she said, "I fell into a state of deep grief when I found that I had been infected two months ago. Now, I have no idea whether I should have children or not." Her voice was choked up with tears. She had just started to work at PDA and was in charge of AIDS education in schools. She said, "At first, it was so painful to talk about my experience in front of students that I was not able to stem the flow of tears. Even though people are afraid of AIDS, I don't want them to avoid people with AIDS."

Prapai, aged 19, holding her handkerchief to her eyes, nodded in agreement. Born into a poor farm family in central Thailand, Prapai went to Bangkok to work in a factory at the age of 15. After a short while, she was sold to a brothel, where she was infected with HIV. She became pregnant, without knowing who the father was, and gave birth. Her baby also had HIV. Her family rejected them, telling her, "We don't want a mother and child with HIV to come home." They were accepted by a private shelter located in a suburb of Bangkok. Shaking my hand in farewell, Prapai murmured, "It is hard for me even to go on living, but I find my reason for living by working in AIDS prevention education. I want to warn women in Japan. If their husbands go overseas to play without any protection, those women will become just like me."

I met Prapai again at the shelter the next year. She has not got AIDS yet, but she looked so lonely that I found myself hugging her. By that time, her baby had already died. The director of the shelter said,

> I went to see the prime minister to request him to set up proper
> HIV/AIDS prevention and care. I wanted to have the prime minister
> hold Prapai's baby. The moment I held out her baby to him, he
> stepped back. But then, he seemed to realize what he had done. Her
> baby contributed to AIDS awareness before it died.

The director sounded as if she were trying to console Prapai.
Prostitution, HIV, the death of her baby, persecuted by her family,
isolated and living in loneliness in the shelter, fearing death: Prapai
has suffered more than any woman, not yet 20 years old, should
have to endure. I wonder if Prapai is still alive.

Brothels are "Detention Centres for Condemned Criminals"

The routes of drugs, prostitution and HIV/AIDS overlap. Northern
Thailand is one such intersection and is at the centre of HIV infection. Sompop Jantonaka, director of the Daughters' Education Programme in Maesai, a town on the northern Thailand–Burma border,
is seriously concerned about 12-year-old Buka, a girl from the Aka
hill tribe. He pointed to a photo of a beautiful girl dressed in black
and red traditional tribal clothing who had tears in her eyes, saying,

> Buka was infected with HIV at a brothel on Pukhet Island, known as
> a "paradise island" resort in southern Thailand. She was sent back to
> her home village in the mountains, a place so poor that people don't
> even have enough food to eat. There is no doctor in the village, so of
> course she cannot receive treatment, and soon she will become ill
> with AIDS. We have no idea how many more years she can live.

All seventeen girls who were in the same brothel as Buka were from
the Aka tribe. Their ages ranged from 11 to 17 years old, and among
them was a 15-year-old girl who was made pregnant.

Sompop also talked about the police raid of three brothels in the
Bangkok area. Some two hundred women in the brothels were
rescued, and thirty-seven of the fifty-five girls who were sent back
home to Maesai village were HIV positive. Most of the girls be-
longed to the hill tribes or were Burmese. Sompop added, "There
are more than fifty brothels in Maesai alone. Ninety per cent of the
girls working there are minors, and many of them are HIV positive."

The reason why young girls from hill tribes are sought is the increased demand for girls who are not yet infected with HIV. However, these girls become infected by their customers within a short period of time.

Professor Vicharn Vitiyasai of Chiang Mai University is investigating the AIDS situation from the period when the Thai government concealed the reality of AIDS, fearing its effect on tourism. The majority of HIV-positive people in northern Thailand are women working in prostitution, and between 60 and 70 per cent of them are girls from hill tribes. This occurs because they are the ones who are most often sent to the lowest-ranked brothels.

Professor Vicharn's investigation shows that the incidence of HIV infection within one year reaches 72.2 per cent of women working at brothels where prostitution fees are under 50 bahts (about US$1), 30.7 per cent at brothels where fees are under 100 bahts, and only 16.7 per cent in brothels where fees are over 100 bahts. This result shows that the poorer women are, the more likely they are to become victims. The women in the cheapest brothels do not know how to protect themselves by making their customers use condoms. They are forced to take about five customers per day, and as many as thirty customers on holidays. Their immature bodies are easily damaged and infected with HIV. Brothels are even called "detention centres for condemned criminals".

> Tourism in northern Thailand first developed in Chiang Mai, the second largest city of Thailand. Next was the ancient city of Chiang Rai, where a new international airport had just been opened, resulting in a tourism boom. Chiang Rai is located close to the "Golden Triangle", which serves as the entrance to Laos, Burma and the southern part of China. The drastic increase in the number of foreign tourists caused huge growth in prostitution in northern Thailand and an accompanying increase in HIV infection.

Professor Vicharn also pointed out the problem of Thai men's habitual use of prostitutes. He emphasized that,

> In Thai society, boys begin to buy women when they are around 13 years old; 50 per cent of 16-year-old boys and 90 per cent of university students go to brothels. Married men also think it natural to entertain business clients and friends by taking them to brothels, and they visit brothels themselves as a part of the joy of travel. We cannot

prevent the spread of HIV infection unless we change Thai men's sexual behaviour.

It is said that 6.2 per cent of all young men in the northern part of Thailand who join the military are infected with HIV.

I met many scholars and medical doctors while I was covering the issue of AIDS in Thailand. Most of them confirmed that "prostitution is the sexual custom of Asian men", but emphasized the absolute necessity of condom use. Only Professor Vicharn questioned prostitution *per se*.

Increase in Mother–Child Infection

The increase in HIV infection is not limited to the northern part of Thailand; it is spreading throughout the nation, with the number of people who are HIV-positive estimated at over one million. It is said that the increased migration of labourers from villages to cities as a result of rapid economic development, accompanied by the male labourer's participation in prostitution, is one of the causes of the sudden explosion in the number of cases of HIV.

The first confirmed case of HIV in Thailand was in 1984, a gay male who had returned to Thailand from the United States. Following that, the number of people infected with HIV through sharing needles gradually increased. Then, infection through heterosexual intercourse showed a sudden increase, and the reported number of people infected with HIV in this way increased from 188 in 1987, "Visit Thailand Year", to 5,000 within the next year. The total number of people with HIV reached 700,000 by the end of 1995, according to UN AIDS Joint Program statistics, 75 per cent of whom were infected through heterosexual intercourse. The World Health Organization (WHO) estimates that by 1997 25,000 to 150,000 people in Thailand will die from AIDS; by the year 2000, the number of people in Thailand infected with HIV will increase from 2 to 4 million.

For women, mother–child infection poses the greatest threat. Wives infected with HIV by husbands who use prostitutes pass on the infection to their babies. Already 3,000 newborn infants who had been infected in this way were reported in 1993. It is said that the infection rate among pregnant women already exceeds 1 per cent. Furthermore, an estimated 10,000 out of every million new-born babies each year are born of mothers infected with HIV; more than 3,000 babies, about 30 per cent of all newborns, are infected themselves, and the remaining 70 per cent are destined to become AIDS orphans upon the death of their parents.

Mari, aged 23, a housewife in Bangkok, says,

> I heard from a doctor that one out of three babies born of mothers infected with HIV is infected by transmission from its mother. So I am so happy to know that Rek, our second daughter, one-and-a-half, has not been infected. But the hardest part is knowing that I will die and not be able to bring up my two children.

Mari massages the body of her husband, who is as thin as a skeleton and in torment in the last stage of AIDS before death, and worries about what will happen after her own death. The tragedy of Mari's family, reported in the *Bangkok Post* (1 December 1994) is only one example of what is happening in Thailand. AIDS is robbing the Thai family of the lives of the next generation and its future.

AIDS, Poverty and Discrimination

Caught in the midst of the national AIDS crisis, Thailand has ad-dressed the issue in various ways, including education via television and posters, village seminars, hospital counselling services, hospice care at Buddhist temples, NGO support programmes for people with HIV, and so on. AIDS prevention education for elementary school students, implemented in northern Thailand in 1990, has spread throughout the nation. I visited an elementary school in a village thirty kilometres east of Chiang Rai. Fourth-grade students were receiving AIDS education in a bamboo-and-wood simple school building erected by villagers. Three young teachers talked enthusi-astically about the importance of educating parents.

> It is important to teach how dreadful AIDS is, but the fundamental solution is to stop trafficking in women. We tell the parents that sending their daughters to the cities is the same as killing them. We appeal to the parents to improve village life so that their daughters can remain in this village.

Many quilts in vivid colours decorated the walls of the office at EMPOWER, a women's organization in Bangkok. These are memorial quilts to honour the memory of friends who had died of AIDS. Chantawipa Apisk, the director of EMPOWER, is actively engaged in conducting AIDS education and is often invited to speak on this topic abroad. She said,

> We focus on AIDS education for women in the sex industry. Our goal is to empower women to protect themselves from AIDS and to live with people with AIDS. We distribute pamphlets with pictures and encourage the performance of dramas which the women themselves write and perform to empower women.

EMPOWER also emphasizes education for young men in the community. One of the staff is a healthy-looking man with HIV, who says, "I was a soccer player. Since I became infected with HIV, I have been visiting high schools and universities to appeal to young people to protect themselves."

Thus, women's organizations are playing a vital role in the battle against AIDS, but the method of approaching the issue varies. Some organizations, such as the shelter where Prapai is living, help HIV-positive people out of charity. The second approach, adopted by EMPOWER and the Foundation for Women, emphasizes the rights and self-reliance of women in prostitution. The third approach includes an increasing number of women's groups which are challenging the prostitution industry and gender discrimination itself in Thai society. They are engaged in a campaign that declares that trafficking in women and prostitution are the primary causes of the spread of AIDS, saying, "Don't sell women. Don't buy women!"

Professor Virada of Chiang Mai University recommends concentrating on limiting the growth of the prostitution industry in Thai society:

> Some women's groups are providing condoms to labourers who are working in cities. But it looks like they are encouraging them to go to brothels. It might be better if they distributed condoms to the men at the entrance of brothels, or even better, if they distributed condoms to women rather than men. We feel the first task is to campaign to stop prostitution. It is unfortunate that some women's groups avoid the issue of prostitution. Just like fighting trafficking in women, so the fight against AIDS is a fight against poverty and discrimination against women.

The Children's Rights Protection Centre in Bangkok, which addresses child prostitution, has started a movement to change the traditional culture of sex, in which prostitution is deeply ingrained, by making and distributing stickers that say, "Young people, do not go to brothels!"

The Spread of AIDS to Neighbouring Countries

HIV infection has also been spreading rapidly in neighbouring countries which send women to Thailand, including Burma, with the number of carriers reaching 200,000. It is estimated that the rate of HIV infection among Burmese girls in Thai brothels is three times that of Thai women, as the Burmese girls are made sex slaves in the poorest brothels. When I went to Thailand on an assignment in 1991, I learned that about a hundred girls had been taken into protection from brothels in a suburb of Bangkok. Twenty were Burmese and, to my surprise, as many as nineteen of them were infected with HIV. Human rights organizations abroad criticize the Thai government for its violation of human rights in forcing HIV tests on Burmese women in brothels without their permission and deporting HIV-positive women back to Burma, now governed by a military administration. WHO is also concerned about the explosion of HIV infection in Burma; however, the exact situation is difficult to ascertain due to the difficulty of getting accurate information from the military regime. Little is known about what happened to those HIV-positive girls deported from Thailand to Burma; there are rumours that they might have been killed when they returned to Burma, but this is difficult to confirm. Nevertheless, it is clear that many girls have contracted AIDS, suffered and died at a very young age without receiving medical treatment or care.

The coming of the United Nations Peacekeeping Operation (PKO), including Japan Self Defence Forces personnel, to Cambodia in 1992 resulted in a brothel area being set up in Phnom Penh. Furthermore, child prostitution has become rampant due to the increased number of foreign businessmen, especially Chinese men, who are asking for young girls in Cambodia, following the introduction of the open-market economy, according to the testimony of Kien Serey Phal, president of the Cambodian Women's Development Association, at the Asian Tribunal on Women's Human Rights in Tokyo in 1994. Consequently, AIDS was also brought into Cambodia, and the hundreds of known cases of HIV infection were confirmed. But

Serey Phal is concerned that the number of known cases of HIV might represent only the tip of the iceberg, given the inadequate testing facilities.

At the end of 1992, I visited Phnom Penh. I saw many heavily made-up young girls with Caucasian men in restaurants and other places. I heard that some of these men were on the staff of NGOs engaged in development assistance.

AIDS is also an urgent issue in Vietnam, Laos and the Yung Nang Province of southern China. These areas also are confronting the interrelated problems of trafficking in women and AIDS which have accompanied the transition to a market economy.

India: A Centre of HIV Infection

India is the Asian country with the largest number of HIV-infected people. It is reported that 80 per cent of HIV transmissions are made through heterosexual intercourse, and the remaining cases are through blood transfusions and drug injections. HIV infection has spread rapidly since the first case: a woman working in a brothel in Madras, who was confirmed as HIV-positive in 1987. The number of HIV-positive cases in India reached 1.75 million by the end of 1995 (UN AIDS Joint Program). It is predicted that by the year 2000, as many as 30 per cent of all of the hospital beds in India may be occupied by AIDS patients.

The situation in Asia is critical, as the number of people with HIV has already reached 4 million (UN AIDS Joint Program) and it will soon surpass that of Africa. India has the largest total number of people infected with HIV in absolute numbers, but Thailand has the highest rate of infection in terms of population ratio. A local university hospital reports that 35 to 40 per cent of the 100,000 women working in prostitution in the brothel area in Bombay, known as the largest brothel area in the world, are infected. The situation is similar in Madras, where some 50,000 women work in brothels. In both cases, Nepalese women are among those victimized. Renu Rajibandri, director of the Women's Rehabilitation Centre in Kathmandu, who conducted a survey in Bombay, reports,

> Thirty-four per cent of Nepalese women working in Bombay brothels were infected because their customers refused to use condoms. We

must provide education to women and demand that customers use condoms. In Bombay, many women continue working after they are infected, which only serves to spread the infection. I fear that the infected women who were deported back to Nepal will be treated brutally.

Efforts by Mighty Nepal

Gita became infected with HIV at a brothel in Bombay. Penniless, she returned home to Nepal in 1991 with the assistance of ABC Nepal, a women's NGO in Kathmandu. Her home is a village in Sindparchowk Province, an area known for trafficking in women. She was accompanied by Dr Pushpa Baht, a woman doctor, who said:

> When we arrived at her village, people in the village, who had already read in a magazine that Gita had been infected with HIV, only glared at her. A neighbourhood teashop even refused to give her a cup of water. This was her first experience of contempt and exclusion. Her father ignored and brushed past her when we met him on the way home. Her mother told her to go back to Kathmandu. Gita burst into tears.

Dr Baht explained about AIDS to Gita's family and relatives, and tried to convince them to accept her. Only her uncle, who is a healer, understood and supported Gita. Concerned about Gita, Dr Baht visited the village a month later. Gita was prohibited from walking on the roads and coming to the market. She was not allowed to share the same eating utensils as her family or so much as touch her siblings. No one showed her the least bit of affection and she had become depressed. Dr Baht said, "She was sold to work in prostitution in Bombay for eleven years. Because of her sacrifice, her family was able to build a house, buy land and support many siblings. In return, this is the way her family treated her. Her uncle told me that she had attempted suicide." Dr Baht pleaded with her uncle, who was the only person who understood Gita, to encourage her and try to convince the people in the village to accept her.

When Dr Baht visited her village six months later, Gita had recovered from her depression, because the village had finally accepted her, thanks to her uncle's persistent efforts. Gita was able to open a small teashop, where she provided AIDS education and health education to customers. Gita cheerfully greeted Dr Baht, saying, "I am all right now! I am even planning to adopt my younger sister's child." Dr Baht wrote up this experience in her journals as follows:

> We can solve the problem, if we persist in working with the infected persons, the family and the local community. It is here that co-operation between NGOs and the community is vital in order to achieve our goal.

Mighty Nepal, an NGO in Kathmandu, accepts women sent back to Nepal from Bombay who are not allowed to return to their villages. The women at Mighty Nepal earn money by making and selling pictures drawn on cloth rather than by sewing, as one drop of blood from a needle prick may become a source of infection. Thus, women's groups are addressing this critical issue in various ways. Trafficking of Nepalese Girls, a booklet published by ABC Nepal, strongly criticizes the government's lack of involvement in preventing the spread of HIV, declaring,

> Poverty is the fundamental cause of the spread of HIV infection in Nepal. Poverty produces an increase of trafficking in women and male migrant workers. Consequently, those who are the most likely to be infected are persons in the remote poverty-stricken mountain villages, causing poor families with HIV-infected family members to sink even deeper into poverty. In addition, the market economy brings an increase in Nepalese businessmen going to Bangkok, and foreign tourists. However, the government has been so slow in adopting measures to deal with the situation that now it cannot alleviate the situation.

Therefore women in the private sector are the ones who are leading the fight against AIDS.

HIV/AIDS has invaded Asia and is attacking the most poverty-stricken women. The pain and suffering of each victim is intense, but the power of women to fight against AIDS in each country is steadily gaining strength.

Chapter 3

The Feminization of
International Migration

An Indonesian Woman's Testimony

"I am Tina, a 26-year-old Indonesian woman. I went to Saudi Arabia and Hong Kong to work, and I had a painful experience there. Six hundred thousand other Indonesian women have had similar experiences", testified Tina, a slender, tiny woman, at the Asian Women's Tribunal, held at Chulalongkorn University in Bangkok in December 1994.

Tina did not have a job when she graduated from high school. Seeing the flyer of an overseas migrant-labour recruitment agency, she applied for a job and was sent to Saudi Arabia. She said, "Since I heard that there was a lot of sexual violence including rape and unwanted pregnancy in Saudi Arabia, I really wanted to go to Hong Kong." Hired as a maid by a Saudi Arabian family with five children, Tina's job began at 6.00 a.m. each morning and she was given no holidays.

Following Islamic custom, which allows polygamy, Tina's employer married a second wife a year later and ordered Tina to work in both wives' households. Tina was not only exhausted from the heavy work; she was also battered and kicked by the first wife, who did not want her to work for the second wife.

> I just couldn't take it any more. In tears, I got a knife from the kitchen and told the first wife that I would rather be killed than battered and kicked. Hearing this, she knocked me down to the floor and dragged me around the room. I escaped into a bathroom and fainted there.

The next day, Tina decided to return to Indonesia, but she discovered that her passport had been taken from her so she couldn't leave the country. She had no choice but to endure the rough treatment and complete her two-year contract before returning home.

When she finally arrived at Jakarta Airport, she discovered the recruiter was waiting for her. He demanded she pay him 150,000 rupiahs (US$15). Furthermore, she was raped in the car that took her back to her home in eastern Java.

The following year, she went to work in Hong Kong, where her elder sister was working. She glanced at her contract during her flight to Hong Kong: it stated that her monthly salary would be HK$2,800 (US$360) per month, with one day off a week. However, she received only HK$1,000. When she protested to the recruitment agency, the agency threatened her, saying she would be sent back to Indonesia if she protested. In addition, her employer sexually harassed her and threatened that she would be sent back if she told his wife. She was given no days off.

One day, Tina met a Filipino woman, who informed her of her rights in regard to salary and time off as stated in the contract. Tina began by making her employer give her one day off per month. She said,

> One day, my employer's wife got mad because I received several phone calls. I demanded she give me the salary and a day off every week as promised in the contract. We argued until midnight. The next morning, I left my employer's house at 4.00 a.m. and went to the Asian Migrant Centre to ask for help.

Tina's real battle started at that moment. She regained her passport with the help of the Indonesian consulate, and continued to press for her rights through legal means, such as mediation at the Division of Labour, the Labour Court and the District Court. Because her father suddenly became ill, Tina had to return to Indonesia before hearing the final results of her legal appeal. However, her painful experience empowered her and made her aware of her rights. She now works in Indonesia, educating and counselling women who are going abroad to work, to prevent them from being exploited out of ignorance. She said, "The agents only pursue their profits and the governments are cold. We women are the only ones who can protect our rights by gathering information for ourselves."

The Abuse of Migrant Women Workers

The Asian Migrant Centre was opened in 1989 to assist foreign migrant workers who face hardship in Hong Kong and help them organize. This centre focuses on non-Filipino migrant workers since several support organizations for Filipinos already exist.

The number of Indonesian domestic workers in Hong Kong rose to 8,100 in 1994, the second largest after Filipinas, who constitute by far the largest group. Consequently, the number of Indonesian women seeking help is also increasing. The Asian Migrant Centre interviewed fifty-seven women who came seeking help and one hundred other foreign domestic workers for the booklet *No Other Place to Go*. This booklet points out that, in addition to the problems shared with male workers, such as unpaid wages, a portion of their wages being taken by agents, overwork, no days off and passport confiscation, women workers face unique problems, such as sexual violence at the hands of male employers and family members and other human rights' violations. Some women who have become pregnant are then thrown out of their employers' houses or become mentally disturbed and roam around the city. Others even commit suicide because they are unable to tolerate the abuse and isolation.

The number of woman migrant workers who are working in Saudi Arabia has increased since the 1970s, as many Indonesian women want to work in another Muslim country. The situation of these women is worse than that of women in Hong Kong. A report at the Conference on Asian Trafficking, held in Seoul in 1990, stated that the number of suicides in Saudi Arabia due to sexual abuse has risen to eleven. "We are treated as if we are not human", "We are regarded as no more than goods or slaves", declare Indonesian women with one voice.

Why are women going abroad to work in spite of the risk of human rights violations? As reported, "Although Indonesian economic development enables a handful of rich to become even richer, 1 billion of the 1.9 billion population are living below the poverty line" ("Asian Migrant Laborers' Conference Report", Taipei, 1994). The minimum-wage policy sets the minimum daily wage at 2,800 rupiahs (US¢25); only three out of ten job applicants find jobs; and 43 per cent of the working population are underemployed (World Bank, 1993). Furthermore, Indonesia's foreign debt totals US$780 billion. Therefore, the Indonesian government is promoting a policy of exporting labour overseas to alleviate the high unemployment rate and gain foreign currency. Consequently, the number of Indonesian migrant workers in Malaysia has reached 1 million, with half of them being illegal residents, in oil-producing countries such as Saudi Arabia, 500,000; and an increasing number in other countries such as Hong Kong, Taiwan, South Korea, Japan, Singapore and the Netherlands. This occurs because recruitment agencies make huge profits and the Indonesian government gives its tacit approval.

The increase in women migrant workers is phenomenal, with over half of the total number of women migrant workers in many countries being employed as domestic workers. It is reported that because of their subordinate position in Indonesian society and their traditional gender role, women's jobs are limited to four categories: domestic work, factory work, prostitution and overseas migrant work. In the case of domestic workers, monthly salaries in Indonesia range from only about US$13 to $26, but reach $135 overseas (Conference on Asian Trafficking, 1990). Furthermore, due to the increased number of women in East Asian countries other than Japan who receive higher education and have their own careers, there is a greater demand for domestic workers to care for children and elderly persons.

At the Asian Migrant Laborers' Conference in Taipei, a representative from Indonesia issued a strong appeal, saying,

> No matter how much we try to stop overseas migration, we cannot solve the problem until there are jobs available at home. The most important thing is to organize migrant workers so that they can protect themselves from exploitation. We need the support of NGOs to achieve this!

The Feminization of Migrant Labour

The era of overseas migrant labour has arrived, with some 1 billion people, the largest number in history, crossing national borders. The rapid increase of overseas migrant workers in Asia is striking, with their number now reaching 13 million.

The first wave of Asian migrant workers to the Persian Gulf oil-producing countries in the Middle East, due to the labour demand of the oil boom, took place in the 1970s, with the number reaching

3.9 million in 1985. The sending countries were originally those surrounding the Persian Gulf, but the range expanded to include those of South Asia and Southeast Asia. Job openings included construction work for men and domestic work, as well as professional occupations such as nurses and teachers, for women.

The second wave of migrant workers, in the 1980s, headed for countries in East Asia undergoing rapid economic development, such as Japan and the NIEs such as South Korea, Taiwan, Hong Kong and Singapore. Due to the expansion of the service sector, the low rate of population increase and the phenomenon of ageing, these countries experienced a labour shortage, especially in the "difficult, dirty, and dangerous" job areas. Malaysia, which is following close behind the NIEs, has also become a receiving country. Thailand is both a sending and a receiving country: migrant workers come from neighbouring countries such as Burma (Myanmar).

The feminization of overseas migrant labour is noticeable, with the number of overseas women migrant workers surpassing that of men from the 1980s. Furthermore, 72 per cent of women migrant workers in the world are Asian (1995 report of Radhika Coomaraswamy, UN Special Rapporteur on Violence against Women). Unique to Asian women's migrant labour is the fact that the main job categories are domestic worker and sex industry worker, as seen in the case of Filipina migrant workers.

The Philippines as a Sending Country

On any Sunday in Hong Kong, the parks overflow with young Filipino women, as does the cathedral close to the park where Filipinas attending mass can be seen crying as they pray. Cynthia Torres, from the Mission to Filipino Migrant Workers in Hong Kong, reports,

> Susie was raped by her employer one night. She had black-and-blue marks all over her body when she ran away from her employer's house. Although she was told that no one would believe her story because her employer was a person of status in Hong Kong society, she pressed charges against him. Her case was dismissed due to insufficient evidence. Many women have such painful experiences simply because they are women. Many recover from the trauma, but some who cannot are hospitalized in psychiatric hospitals.

In Hong Kong, some 100,000 Filipino domestic workers, known as amah, suffer exploitation and sexual violence similar to that of Indonesian domestic workers.

Some 60,000 Filipinas are working in Singapore. Flor Contemprasion, aged 42, the mother of four children, and another maid were sentenced to death for the murder of their employer's child. They were executed in March 1995, despite a campaign in the Philippines and throughout the world appealing for the commuting of the death sentence. Six months later, 16 year old Sara Barabagan was sentenced to death for the murder of her employer. A Muslim Moro from Mindanao, Sara was threatened with a knife and raped by her 80-year-old employer, also a Muslim. Enraged, she wrested the knife from her employer and stabbed him thirty-four times. "Why should a rape victim be sentenced to death?" Testimonies of protest and support were voiced throughout the world. Filipino women demonstrated at home and in Hong Kong as well. As a result, Sara's sentence was reduced to 100 lashes, one year's imprisonment and compensation to be paid to the victim's family in a judgement handed down in October 1995. These two cases served to focus international attention on violence against women who are in a weak position as domestic workers.

The Philippines is the number-one migrant-labour-exporting country, sending 3.5 million migrant workers to 135 countries. The workers send home US$3 billion annually, which serves as the country's main source of foreign currency. With 60 per cent of the population existing below the poverty line, an unemployment rate of 11.6 per cent and foreign debt of a $30 billion, labour exportation, which has been a national policy in the Philippines since the Marcos administration, has continued to increase.

Sixty-five per cent of Filipino migrant workers overseas are women; even the percentage of women migrant workers going to Saudi Arabia, once the country to which male migrant workers were sent, has risen to 55 per cent of the total. Besides the human rights violations experienced by the female migrant workers, the long separations from their children and their families must be considered.

Japan has become more and more important as the receiving country of Filipina migrant workers, although the job description is almost totally limited to that of entertainer. While Thai women are sent to Japan by trafficking agencies as "undocumented workers", many Filipinas come to Japan in a legal capacity as singers or dancers on entertainment visas. The number of Filipinos entering Japan on entertainment visas between 1988 and 1994 exceeded 370,000, most of them women. The total number of women entering Japan on either tourist or entertainment visas who overstay their visas includes between 700,000 and 800,000 Filipinas per year who work in the expanding sex industry. Even many of those who hold entertainment visas are forced to serve alcoholic beverages to customers as hostesses in bars and engage in prostitution, earning a little extra because their monthly salary is only about US$500. In addition, they are under the control of Japanese organized crime.

Maripel's Funeral

The funeral of Maripel, a 20-year-old Filipino woman, took place on 29 June 1992, in a Catholic church in Tokyo. It was a morning when the city was caught up in the festivities related to the wedding of a young Japanese woman to the emperor's second son. When Maripel came to Japan a year after her father's death, she was 17 years old. Her passport bore a false name and age, listing her as 22, five years older than her actual age. She moved around from place to place, working in snack bars and nightclubs, sending money home to her impoverished, fatherless family for her siblings' school fees.

Probably due to loneliness, two months earlier Maripel had moved in with a man, whose body was covered with tattoos; he battered her to death. Her mother, who came to Japan for the funeral and to claim her daughter's ashes, dissolved into tears when she saw her daughter for the first time in three years. She was shocked at the change that had taken place in the appearance of her daughter's now lifeless body. Maripel's false name and age were written in Japanese on the urn that contained her remains. The sight of the mother as she left the crematorium clutching her daughter's urn and staggering down the steps formed a stark contrast to the otherwise happy atmosphere of the city. To what extent do Japanese people realize the human rights violations that lie behind Japan's prosperity?

Not only Filipino women but also other Asian women continue to suffer painful deaths in Japan, resulting from murder, suicide, accidents and malnutrition. In the spring of 1994, the Asian Tribunal on Women's Human Rights was held in Tokyo. The night before the tribunal, a Night of Mourning for the Victims of Sexual Violence was held. A candlelit procession moved through the crowded, neon-lit streets of Shibuya, Tokyo, to honour the young women who have died in far-off foreign countries. The list of victims compiled for the Night of Mourning from newspapers, support organizations and embassies included approximately one hundred women from various Asian countries who have died violently from stabbing, strangulation and immolation, and the suicides of eight Filipino women over a two-year period.

The poem "Requiem for the Crushed Flowers", read by Itsuko Ishikawa at the Night of Mourning for the Victims of Sexual Violence, mourns the spirits of young women forced to serve as "comfort women", victims of Japanese military sexual slavery, who never returned home, as well as women like Maripel who have been killed by the sex industry, a modern form of sexual slavery.

> We will never forget
> The mortification, the sadness you bore
> For we are also women
> We, too, can feel your pain
> Why did they tear you asunder
> Why did they crush you down
> Turning the flower so fair
> Into bones so icy cold
> We will carry your appeal, your message
> To the ends and the depths of the earth.

Expanding Support Activities

Asian women are not only victims. In my contact with support networks in various locations throughout Japan, including shelters and counselling programmes, I am amazed by the strength of the Filipino women. I am impressed both with the great vitality of the entertainers who wish to return home as *panaros* (successful people), carrying large sums of money they have earned, and with the strength of Filipino women married to Japanese men (marriages between Filipino women and Japanese men have steadily increased since the 1980s), and their ability to deal with the loneliness of living in a foreign country by forming their own groups, publishing newsletters and organizing social events.

I was impressed by the cheerful atmosphere when I visited Bethune House, a shelter for Filipino women in Hong Kong. This centre was established by a young Filipino missionary couple, Jun and Cynthia Torres, in memory of their only daughter, Bethune, who died in a traffic accident. There were about twenty women at the centre: domestic workers who had escaped from abuse and exploitation such as violence, sexual harassment and unpaid wages.

When I visited the centre, they were holding a farewell dinner party for a Swedish woman who had supported the centre both financially and emotionally. After dinner, everyone sang songs like "Starved Peasants" and "We Are Also Human Beings." Mars, one of three centre staff and a social worker, accompanied the singing on her guitar. The Swedish volunteer said to me, "When women bearing both emotional and physical wounds come to the centre, Mars listens to and consoles them, sometimes even all night long, helping them to recover from their trauma."

Buhai, another member of staff, started to dance, her entire body gently swaying, keeping time with the music. Buhai had come to Hong Kong as a domestic worker about ten years previously, and suffered abuse. As soon as it opened, she rushed to the centre seeking help, and later began to work there. I heard that a Filipino poet who visited the centre was so impressed by her that he composed a poem in honour of women who work hard so far away from home. The poem was set to beautiful music, and we joined together to sing that song. The staff are always thinking about how to empower the survivors who come to Bethune House, not how to control them. In so doing, empowered survivors have become staff. I found this to be an independent, equal, open Filipino democracy.

The final song we sang was "Mother, Please Come Home", composed by 40-year-old Nars, whose understanding employer lets her come to the centre to work as a volunteer on her days off. Her daughter at home in the Philippines has just turned 18, and the song communicates her daughter's feelings.

> Mother, why must you cross the ocean
> To gain a bright future?
> Mother, you can't realize your dream in this country,
> The dream to gain your freedom.

Mother, please come home!
Please stay by my side!
I want to feel your kiss, your arms embracing me,
Even if we cannot realize our dream in this country
We can be happy as long as we are together,
For you are the guiding hand of my life!

The songs sung by these women through their tears communicate the protest of millions of women who must go abroad to work, robbed of their right to live with their families in their own countries. They are threatened by poverty, which is intensified by the globalization increasing the gap between countries of the South and the North.

May Ann Villalba, a member of the Asian Migrant Centre staff, analyses the situation as follows:

The structure in which developing countries supply the demand by the NIEs for domestic workers and the demand by Japan for entertainers is based on the male-centred Asian value system that simply regards women as objects existing for the purpose of domestic work or sex, has promoted women migrant labour. Industrialized countries' exploitation of the Third World and the skewed development among Asian countries are also promoting increased feminization of migrant labour.

The problems related to Asian women migrant workers will not be solved until discrimination against women is eliminated and the unfair economic system is changed. It is essential to strengthen support activities to protect these women's human rights on a daily basis.

Chapter 4

Japanese-Filipino Children and Japanese Society

Mariko's Dream

The problem of Japanese-Filipino Children (JFC) abandoned by their Japanese fathers first surfaced as an issue in Japan when the director of Batis Centre came to Japan in the spring of 1993. The Batis Centre, a women's NGO in Manila, supports Filipino women who return from Japan. The Batis Centre director travelled around Japan searching for the Japanese fathers of Japanese-Filipino children. In January 1994, I went to the Philippines and, for the first time, became aware of the real situations of these mothers and children.

Stumbling along a bumpy road, my feet mired down in mud, I reached 15-year-old Mariko's home, a one-room apartment in a Manila suburb. I was captivated by the warm smile of Mariko's mother, 40-year-old Lilia, when she opened the door, realizing what a difficult life she must have endured. Lilia was working at a restaurant in Manila when she met a Japanese man who was working in a job related to Japanese economic aid. He hired her as a maid and then made her pregnant. The man said "Get an abortion!" and gave her 3,000 pesos (US$70). He returned to Japan and married a Japanese woman the following year. Lilia gave birth to Mariko in a Catholic country that frowns upon abortion. Lilia said, "At the time, I was angry with him; I felt bitter and humiliated. I was ashamed of being a single mother. But I reconsidered and decided that I was responsible for bringing up Mariko in the very best way I could." Lilia is now making a living by peddling underwear door to door and doing other odd jobs. This mother and her daughter are living an austere life, having only two beds and a few kitchen utensils in the corner of their room. Listening to her mother's story, Mariko said,

> I was shocked when my mother told me that my father was Japanese and that he had deserted us. But I feel immense sympathy for my mother, who was betrayed by my father, and I am deeply grateful to my mother who has struggled so hard to raise me by herself. I am proud of my mother, who has struggled and overcome this hardship. I want to go to college so I can help my mother.

Mariko is studying very hard and always gets top grades at school. "The older I become, the more I want to see my father. I wrote a letter to him in English, but I didn't receive a reply. I want to meet him; even just once is OK. This is my dream."

In May 1994, Mariko visited Japan by invitation of the International Children's Rights Centre, an Osaka support group for Japanese-Filipino children. She gave an outstanding speech at a symposium in Tokyo.

> My mother has never spoken ill of my father. I want to see and hug my father even just once. I have grown up with my loving mother and will always be grateful to her. But we also need to find our other roots. I want to take home hope and dreams to the children in the Philippines like me. We do not need your pity, but your action to change the situation!

Symposium participants, moved by Mariko's appeal, decided to organize the Citizens' Network for Japanese-Filipino Children (JFC). I am chairperson of this network.

Mariko's dream came true. She was able to meet her father. But I heard that she did not give him the T-shirt which she had brought for him because she was concerned about the problem it might cause his family, since he has children the same age as Mariko. When I heard this, I felt that she was a more mature human being than her father. I recalled the words of Filipino Catholic Cardinal Sin, who says, "The Japanese have money. The Filipinos have smiles!"

The Mothers' Appeal

In September I participated in the JFC network field survey tour, and in January I visited about ten JFC families. The poverty of these families was what struck me most during these two tours. In many cases, the mothers met the Japanese men who had made them pregnant while they were working in Japan. These women are all from impoverished families. In addition, it is hard for them both to work and to care for their children; they are caught in extreme poverty.

I visited a mother and child living in a slum in Angeles, the site of the former USAF Clark Base, about one hour from Manila. Passing under laundry hanging from poles, I threaded my way down a narrow alley to a house at the very end. In the living room, the floor of which seemed about to collapse, I found a pale-complexioned woman, surrounded by many family members. She sat holding a skinny girl who looked Japanese. I was told that ten people were living in this humble house. Twenty-year-old Jasmin seemed fatigued as she spoke,

> There were fourteen children in our family. Our father died, and although our mother works very hard to support us by taking in laundry and doing odd jobs, our life is still very hard, so I went to Japan to work when I was 17 years old. I dated a Japanese man who was a customer where I worked. I came back home because I was pregnant, and I had a baby the year before last. Then I stopped hearing from him. Even when I asked him to send money for our child, he never responded. He seems to have another Filipino woman now. I started working at a karaoke bar recently because I don't even have money for my baby's milk.
>
> My life is as good as over, but I do not want my child to experience the same kind of misery. I want her to go to school. All I want is for her father to send money for school fees. But I don't even know his address. Please help me find him!

This was the desperate appeal of a poor mother whose only hope lies in her child.

I visited 35-year-old Yolanda in Tarlac, where the volcanic ash from the eruption of Mount Pinatubo is still evident. She sat, her large body in a wheelchair, with her 4-year-old daughter, Yoriko standing by her side. Yolanda went to Japan to work on several occasions, from the time she was 24 years old, to support her large family. Yolanda was hired by a production agency in Manila, run by a Japanese man who came and went between the Philippines and Japan; that man is the father of Yoriko. When he attended Yoriko's baptism, the father got mad over some trifle and returned to Japan.

After that, no matter how many times Yolanda tried to make contact with him, she never heard from him. Having a newborn baby, Yolanda felt desperate. She attempted suicide, shooting herself with a pistol. Although her life was spared, she suffers from the after-effects, and the lower half of her body is now paralysed. When she first came to Batis Centre, she could only shed tears over the deep wound she bore in her heart. Her life became even more difficult due to her physical disability. She wants Yoriko's father to acknowledge his daughter and at least pay the expense of rearing her. However, not even the Japanese lawyer has been able to make contact with Yoriko's father.

Later, when I visited Yolanda with a social worker from Batis Centre, she looked a little better than before. She was making a living by selling food. When I visited her a third time, when I was in the Philippines on a field survey, she even smiled occasionally as she sat in her worn-out wheelchair. Little Yoriko is Yolanda's life support. Although she is not yet even 5 years old, she is considerate of her mother, saying in all innocence, "Because my father does not buy medicine for her, she has not got well yet. When I grow up, I will become a doctor and make her walk again."

All of the mothers of JFC are living with pain in their hearts. They expressed humiliation at not being treated as human beings and a sense that Japanese men are betraying women by selfishly concealing that they are married, irresponsibly abandoning their wives and children, or treating Filipino women, especially entertainers, with contempt. The women wonder whether these Japanese men have ever known such pain or whether they will not acknowledge it even if it exists.

The Children's Pain

Twelve-year-old Ryuji lives in a large house in a suburb of Manila. He looks Japanese. Ryuji's mother, 30-year-old Julietta, met a 53-year-old Japanese real estate agent in Tokyo while she was working in Japan. Their official marriage was registered in the Philippines, where Ryuji was born. But this man already had a family in Japan, so he was committing bigamy. Ryuji showed me his precious photo album, saying, "Mom has gone to Japan again to work." The album contained various pictures haphazardly pasted in, including photos of Ryuji at a young age with his father, and of his mother when she was working in Japan.

The father who used to come to visit Ryuji frequently suddenly stopped coming when he was around 5 years old. Ryuji said,

> When I was little, my father took me lots of places and bought me many things. When he came to Manila the last time, I was so happy to see him at the airport, I ran to him. But when he said "don't bother me", and pushed me away, I felt so sad. Since then, he has never come to see me. I felt lonely, and I wrote many letters to him, but he never answered them. I don't write him anymore. At school, more than anything else, I hate it when people say, 'Your mother has gone to Japan to work as a *Japayuki!*' [discriminatory term used to refer to migrant women working in the Japanese sex industry]. I am studying hard, because I want to be a computer engineer and help my mother so that she doesn't have to go to Japan anymore.

Although bearing deep wounds, Ryuji adores his mother and tries to be brave.

On the other hand, some children feel hatred toward their fathers. Eight-year-old Taro picks fights, grabbing at children who pick on him and say, "Bastard! Your Japanese father must be bald!" One night, Taro said to his mother, "If I ever meet my father, I will hit him! I will shoot him with a gun!" His mother left home with Taro and his younger brother Tomoki when Taro's father brought home another woman. Taro's mother supported them, working as a laundry woman or street vendor; at times, she has had to leave her children in a children's home. Then she married a Filipino man, but the man's parents said to Taro and his brother, "You are sons of a Japanese." They looked down on the two boys and abused them. Finally, Taro's mother and her two children were driven out of the home. They now live in a squatter area, and Taro is not even able to go to school, which only increases his hatred for his Japanese father. This case was reported in a local newspaper. All the children who have been abandoned by their Japanese fathers hold a grudge against them. The only difference among the children is whether they maintain their resentment or can somehow manage to overcome it.

Michelle, 14, is one of three Japanese-Filipino children who came to Japan in May 1995. She made her appeal in tears:

When my father refused to acknowledge that I am his daughter, I was deeply hurt and I cried for many days. I felt great anger toward my father. But then I came to realize that he must have had some reasons for abandoning me, so then I decided to try to see the good side of him. No matter what kind of person he is, he is still my father. So, no matter what, I want to meet him.

Michelle was able to meet her father just before she left Japan.

On the other hand, Shinichi, 11, was not able to meet his father, and was only able to speak with him by phone. Shinichi declares, "I am studying very hard so I can become a lawyer and work for JFC in the future. I have never seen my father's face, and he has refused to acknowledge me as his son, but I love him, and so I want to meet him." Because of his deep disappointment, he has experienced emotional problems since returning to the Philippines.

Another JFC, Akiko, 11, said in tears, "Because JFC have been deserted by their fathers and feel such pain, I don't want little children who are not able to understand such things to grow up experiencing the pain and sadness that we have experienced." She is teased and called "child of a prostitute in Japan". Akiko frequently expressed words of encouragement to victims of the great Kobe earthquake when she came to Japan, as if she somehow shared their pain, saying, "I saw the after-effects of the earthquake in Kobe and Osaka. I can understand the pain of losing your family members. Please continue to live without losing your hope!"

The three JFC who came to Japan repeated the words "Thank you" many times. They expressed their thanks to "Mother, who has struggled to raise me alone", "Father, who was willing to meet me", "Kind Japanese friends", "Japanese people who have supported me", and "God". I feel great respect for their mothers, who have raised such sensitive children in spite of the abuse they have suffered from Japanese men and their difficult struggle to survive.

Double Discrimination

The number of JFC abandoned by their Japanese fathers is estimated to be over ten thousand. I noticed children who looked Japanese everywhere I went in the Philippines. According to a Batis Centre survey of 130 children in 113 cases who have come to the Batis

Centre, approximately 70 per cent of the JFC are children born to Filipino women working in Japan in bars or clubs and their Japanese customers or Japanese club employees; some 20 per cent are children born to women working in bars or clubs in the Philippines and Japanese resident businessmen or tourists; and about 10 per cent are children born to Japanese–Filipino couples introduced by marriage agencies or friends. Of these couples, approximately 60 per cent are unmarried and about 20 per cent are married but have registered the marriage only in the Philippines. Of the married couples, twelve involve bigamy, and only eighteen couples, or a mere 16 per cent, have gone through the legal process of registering the marriage in Japan.

The following pattern emerges as a result of this survey. Japanese men form relationships with Filipino women working in the sex industry. The women who become pregnant return to the Philippines to give birth when their entertainer visas expire, and after a short time the men are not heard from again. These men lose interest in the women as objects of sexual pleasure when the women become mothers. Then they find other women and stop sending money for raising their children. The Filipino women are forced by their employers to attract customers to their bars or clubs. There, as part of a business relationship, they serve customers who show an interest in them. In so doing, the women become unable to distinguish between love and showing hospitality. Furthermore, according to the lawyers involved in JFC issues, they may think that they will receive some financial support and so finally accept these irresponsible Japanese men.

The Japanese men treat Filipino women as they please, taking advantage of the vast gap in economic power between Japan and the Philippines. They epitomize sexism, viewing Filipino women as mere sex objects, and racism, looking down on Filipino people as backward and poor. However, only blaming the fathers does not achieve anything. It is also important to recognize that some of the fathers are men who are dropouts from Japan's competitive society and are members of the lower-income group who tend to be ignored by Japanese women. As such, some of these men are also victims of today's inhumane Japanese society.

The Responsibility of Japanese Citizens

These Filipina mothers, who stand in a very weak position and who have been abandoned along with their children, only seek for the fathers to provide financial support, especially the support needed to raise their children. In order to achieve this, for fathers to acknowledge their children is essential. As for the children, more than anything else they want to meet their fathers.

However, Japan's Immigration Control and Refugee Recognition Act prevents these mothers and children from entering Japan to negotiate with or meet the fathers. This system favours the Japanese men. However, Batis Centre began to address JFC issues in 1993, and a JFC legal team was formed in Japan. In 1994, citizens groups to support JFC sprang up all over Japan. Their activities include searching for fathers, helping mothers to become self-reliant, providing exchanges for Japanese-Filipino children, and lobbying for changes in Japanese laws.

The cold attitude toward these mothers and children is deeply rooted in Japanese society, with some people still saying, "Why should society have to deal with the aftermath of irresponsible couples who should themselves take responsibility? Isn't it a violation of privacy to interfere?" Thus, in only about twenty cases have fathers been found. We need to involve Japanese society more widely in order to achieve a solution to the problems of financial support issues for children and to enable fathers and children to meet.

Concern for human rights serves as the basis for these activities. The UN Convention on the Rights of the Child, finally ratified by the Japanese government in 1994, specifies that every child has the right to be protected from discrimination based on race, social class birth or other status, as well as the individual right to life, the right to claim nationality, the right to know parents, the right to be cared for by parents, the right to maintain contact with parents and the right to establish contact with parents who live in another country. JFC, however, have been robbed of these rights. Isn't it the responsibility of Japanese citizens to restore these rights to children by becoming involved in support activities and pressing their government to implement the terms of the convention?

At the same time, we have to protect the human rights of mothers. The Convention on the Elimination of All Forms of Discrimination against Women, adopted by the United Nations in 1979 and ratified by the Japanese government in 1985, is based on that principle, realizing absolute gender equality and acknowledging the joint responsibility of parents and society in raising children.

Finally, we must make every effort to change Japan's distorted sex culture, which regards women as merely sex objects. As Mariko emphasized, changing the situation requires action, not pity.

Chapter 5

Women Break the Silence on Domestic Violence

Conference on Domestic Violence

Mao Corn was living with her husband, who drove a three-wheeled taxi, in a squatter area in Phnom Penh, the capital of Cambodia. Mao's first husband, whom she married in their rural village, had left for Phnom Penh in search of a job. When he did not return, Mao went to Phnom Penh to look for him. There she collapsed when she became ill, and she later married the kind taxi driver who took her to the hospital. She learned that he had also left his first wife back in his rural village and come to Phnom Penh, having lost all his water buffalo through gambling, so that he was unable to continue farming. She said,

> I may be killed by my husband tonight. My husband's violence began three years after we married. I am his servant and his slave. After he returns from gambling or brothels, he complains about dinner and becomes violent. He beats me, kicks me, lashes me with a rope and clubs me with a thick bamboo pole. I am always covered with wounds and blood. If I cry, he behaves even more brutally. I am ashamed for the neighbours to hear, so I cannot even raise my voice. Recently, he once again threatened me with death. Hearing me complain, "Every day I balance a heavy basket on my head and walk all over the city selling goods, working hard to earn money so that I can feed you, but you only beat me even harder after you eat what I have earned", he tried to choke me, wrapping a cord around my neck, and dragged me outside of our house. My skirt was pulled off in the mud and you could see my bare skin. I felt so humiliated that I rushed into the house and picked up a knife to kill him. We fought with each other until we were both covered with blood. I asked my

neighbours for help. I was beaten on the back with firewood the
night before last, and by an iron pipe yesterday morning. There is
nothing left to do but divorce him!

Mao told her story in a video produced by the Khmer Women's
Voice, the women's group to which Mao fled for her life. Her body
thin and emaciated, her pale face covered with wounds, Mao sobbed
as she poured out her soul. At the end, the narrator said, "One
month after this video was made, Mao committed suicide by hanging herself."

I saw this video tape at the Asia-Pacific Conference on Domestic
Violence, held in Phnom Penh in December 1994. This conference
was jointly sponsored by UNICEF and the Cambodian Ministry on
Women's Issues, in preparation for the Beijing UN Fourth World
Women's Conference. Forty representatives from various Asian
countries and three hundred women from Cambodia assembled to
discuss strategies for eradicating violence.

Cambodia is known as a nation of smiles, and truly the
Cambodian people are very peaceful by nature. However, not only
this video but also the report "Domestic Violence in Cambodia",
submitted to the conference, clearly revealed the hidden reality of
husbands' violence for the first time. The 300-page report contains
the results of a painstaking survey, including interviews with fifty
battered women and the mothers of women killed by husbands.

The report points out the following causes of domestic violence:
(1) the belief that wives have to endure their husbands' violence
because it is a private matter; (2) poverty, gambling, alcohol and
low education levels; (3) gender discrimination and inequality, which
encourages women's subservience to men; (4) the Buddhist concept
that victims' hardships derive from retribution for their behaviour
in a previous life, and a feeling of shame which encourages women
to conceal the problem; (5) the lack of any system to punish abusers;
and (6) the influence of violence under the Pol Pot regime, as a
problem unique to Cambodia.

The report finds that the aftermath of the violence under the Pol
Pot regime, which murdered more than 1 million of the 7 million
Cambodian people, still affects Cambodian families. "Under the era
of Khmer Rouge, the Pol Pot sect, the hearts of Cambodian men
were changed. As a result of the violence he witnessed in those
days, my husband becomes brutal over trifling matters", testifies a

woman whose husband, a former Pol Pot soldier, held an axe to her head. The report describes how the men, traumatized by their daily experience of the bloody massacre, act out their violence on wives who are in a weaker position.

Furthermore, the mass slaughter under the Pol Pot regime has resulted in a population imbalance between men and women; there are currently six women for every four men, which only serves to weaken the position of women further. It is reported that, in many cases, husbands take mistresses and thus abuse their wives, in whom they have lost interest.

Speaking Out about Wife Abuse

Although the situation differs from country to country, women in every country suffer from husbands' violence. In August 1995, a public hearing on domestic violence was held in Colombo, Sri Lanka, sponsored by the Women's Human Rights' Network and the Asia-Pacific Forum on Women's Law and Development. The goal of this hearing was to supply information to Radhika Coomaraswamy, the Sri Lankan woman lawyer appointed to be the UN Special Rapporteur on Violence against Women. Three women victims and representatives from groups supporting women from eight countries attended the hearing.

When 24-year-old Sita from Nepal, a charming young woman dressed in a vividly coloured embroidered shawl, removed her shawl we saw that she had lost both hands. Sita was breastfeeding her baby when her drunken husband attacked her with a sword. As she raised both hands to protect her baby, her husband severed Sita's two hands at the wrists.

Anama, 23, a dark-skinned Malaysian woman of Indian background, bore a deep burn scar on her neck. Her husband, a palm-oil-producing farm labourer, had poured kerosene over her and attempted to burn her to death. She lost consciousness for two weeks; after she recovered from the burns she attempted suicide. Finally, after her husband raped her 11-year-old daughter, Anama left home.

Chong Man Sung, 42, a Korean woman with three children, was raped by a soldier and then, unwillingly, married him. Her husband became violent whenever he drank. She became neurotic and left home many times, but she had no place to go. But when she discovered that her husband had had sexual relations with both her

younger sister and other women, she finally sought refuge at a
shelter.

Support Mechanisms and Legal Advocacy

Although it is very painful for victims to testify in public to their
husbands' violence, the growth of victim support activities, such as
women's counselling programmes and the establishment of shelters,
has made this more possible.

One of the groups participating in the Colombo conference was
the Women's Aid Organization (WAO), the first NGO women's
shelter, established by women in Malaysia in 1982. Women victims,
who had formerly believed that their husbands' violence was a
private issue and so had decided against taking any action, can now
receive telephone counselling and take refuge in the shelter, where
they can receive support. Furthermore, the shelter has also become
a place from which to raise public awareness of other types of
violence against women, including rape and sexual harassment.

After more than a decade of agitation, the women's campaign
finally bore fruit with the passage of a law against domestic violence. "This law, which immediately protects women victims, is
based on the perception of domestic violence as an illegal act against
society, not as a personal issue", stresses Irene Fernandes, an activist
in the movement campaigning against violence against women.

> As a result of this campaign, feminist women's groups acting from
> the perspective of gender have sprung up all over the nation. Differ-
> ent from the traditional women's movement, this movement empha-
> sizes the sisterhood of all women, with women taking action not as
> individuals, but as groups. Shelters and telephone counselling are
> operated not out of charity, but for mutual empowerment by women
> supporting women.

In Korea also, the women's movement has focused on issues of
sexual violence, addressing such issues as "comfort women", rape
and husbands' violence as key concerns. The Korean Women's Hot
Line, established in 1983, has become a place from which to appeal
against husbands' violence, a hidden issue until now. One survey
found that 45 per cent of the 800 women questioned had experienced violence, making it clear that this is a serious social issue. The

Korean Women's Hot Line has trained more than a thousand volunteer hot-line counsellors, established shelters in various parts of the country and become involved in supporting women victims.

In the 1990s, the Korean Women's Hot Line called on twenty-four women's organizations to join together in launching a campaign to establish a law against sexual violence, resulting in the passage of a special law in 1993. Although this law signifies progress in terms of enlarging the definition of sexual violence from rape to include sexual harassment, molestation and the transmission of pornographic messages on the Internet, as well as mandating the establishment of shelters nationwide, it is still far from fulfilling women's demands. Shin Hei Soo, representative of the Korean Women's Hot Line and International Liaison Representative on the "comfort women" issue, states,

> We have to change the present criminal law concept of sexual violence as the breaking of fidelity, and we demand the inclusion of marital rape in this special law, because as women, we consider rape as a violation of women's human rights in terms of self-determination of sexual behavior. The new law does not include the issue of husbands' violence toward wives, so we are continuing our campaign to enact more effective anti-sexual violence legislation.

In Japan, domestic violence, especially husbands' violence toward wives, has not surfaced as an issue compared with other types of sexual violence, such as rape and sexual harassment. However, results of a survey conducted in 1992 by the Husbands' and Partners' Violence against Women Study Group indicate that over half of the 800 women respondents had experienced some form of violence, and approximately 300 respondents had incurred injuries due to this violence. Respondents insisted on the necessity of raising social awareness, increasing support for women victims and implementing more effective legislation as a means of solving problems of violence.

According to the report of the Hot Line on Spousal Violence, conducted by the Japan Bar Association in 1994, 563 out of the 1,249 calls were related to divorce, of which some two-thirds, or 65.8 per cent, reported husbands' violence. The Japan Bar Association analyse the Hot Line calls as follows:

> In Japan, the wives themselves do not perceive husbands' violence as either a human rights issue or a social problem. Wives tend to deal

with husbands' violence as a domestic matter and, furthermore, there
is no existing public policy to address this issue. In addition, women
cannot take action to divorce because they have not achieved financial
self-reliance and they have no access to public assistance.

Sharman Babior, an American woman cultural anthropologist who
conducted research in Japan for her Ph.D. dissertation, "Domestic
Violence and Sexual Exploitation in Japan", points out that "Japanese
women are characterized as having a strong sense of shame, being
reluctant to discuss their problems, and continuing to endure their
pain." How can we change Japanese society, in which women find
it so difficult to raise their voices in the midst of their pain? This
is the challenge that Japan must begin to address.

Female Infanticide

Domestic violence against women is not limited to husbands' violence toward wives. Women are threatened with gender violence
from before birth until old age. Merely being a woman means being
subject to a lifetime of violence, which includes the abortion of
female foetuses based on the result of ultrasound testing, murder,
abandonment, lack of opportunities to receive education, child sexual
abuse, human trafficking by parents and abuse against elderly women.
In societies where boys are perceived to be superior to girls, the
lives of girls are destroyed. India is a country in which there is an
ongoing decline in the ratio of women to men, with the ratio of
women to every 1,000 men dropping from 972 in 1901, to 946 in
1951 and only 929 in 1991. In India, it is customary for brides to
bring dowry to their bridegrooms at the time of marriage. Since the
amount of the dowry is increasing with India's economic development, many families with daughters encounter serious financial
difficulties, which leads to the practice of aborting female foetuses.

With the development of the means of determining the sex of a
foetus, the number of pregnant women receiving this test has drastically increased. It is reported that over the period 1978 to 1983,
78,000 female foetuses were aborted, and the number of abortions
of female foetuses has continued to increase. Women are now
questioning the use of advanced technology for such purposes. However, poor women who cannot afford to have the test to determine
the sex of the foetus have no alternative than to give birth. Conse-

quently, female infanticide has become widespread. A 26-year-old mother stated in an Indian magazine, "The reason why I killed my baby is to save her from lifelong humiliation as a daughter of a poor family that cannot pay a dowry. My husband and I came to the conclusion that death following one or two hours of pain is better than a whole lifetime of pain." This points out clearly the connection between traditional customs that discriminate against women and poverty.

Even if girls can live without being killed at the time of birth, they tend to receive less nourishment than boys. One survey reports that 71 per cent of girls in India suffer from malnutrition, while only 28 per cent of boys do. Furthermore, statistics indicate that the number of girls who are brought to the hospital for medical care is only half that of boys. Consequently, the infant mortality rate of females is higher than that of males in India. Even if they survive, the school enrolment rate for girls is lower than for boys, and even if girls can enter school, many of them cannot continue their education. Such gender discrimination in education makes it more difficult for women to achieve self-reliance and forces them into lifelong subordination.

China's One-Child Policy

In China, a densely populated country of more than 12 billion people, the one-child policy, instituted in 1979, is resulting in female infanticide. Today, a half-century after the 1949 revolution, in spite of the campaign for gender equality conducted through legislation and education, the Confucian philosophy of male superiority remains deep rooted. Especially in agricultural areas, under the one-child policy, the tendency to prefer a boy to a girl is conspicuous.

In 1983, the shocking news of the increase in female infanticide in Guangdong and Anhui Provinces was disseminated so widely throughout the world that the Chinese premier was forced to issue a public denial. Nevertheless, the discrepancy in the birth rates of males and females is increasing. According to a national survey, for every 100 girls born in 1980, 108.5 boys were born; by 1990, this had risen to 111.4 boys. The total number of girls born in 1989 was 600,000 fewer than that of boys. It is thought that this difference results from abortion of female foetuses, immersion of female infants in water to induce suffocation, or female infant births not being officially registered. A researcher on Chinese women points out,

> Before the Revolution, female infanticide was commonplace in China due to poverty and the Confucian tradition that views women as being inferior. However, because infanticide was prohibited by law after the Revolution, female infanticide was rarely practised. Recently, however, the practice of female infanticide has once again been employed because people prefer males, due to the one-child policy.

Furthermore, mothers who bear girls are also abused. Sometimes, husbands treat them violently, mothers-in-law do not give them any food or they are divorced. A tragic case was reported in which a husband, who was disappointed and angry when his wife bore a girl, inserted a firecracker in her vagina. As a researcher on China points out,

> With the Chinese government open reform policy and the introduc-tion of the market economy, which places first priority on efficiency, the system of individual labour contracts was implemented in agricul-tural villages; increasing the demand for boys who would provide agricultural labour. Girls became victims of infanticide or abandon-ment, and trafficking in girls is increasing.

Moreover, recent rapid economic development is escalating violence against women.

Although the specific forms of violence differ from country to country, other Asian countries are also experiencing the increase in violence against women that occurs when a traditional contempt for women is accompanied by a transition to a market economy.

Making the Personal Political

Charlotte Bunch, the American feminist activist who created a sen-sation in the international women's movement by calling for the reconsideration of human rights issues from a gender perspective and the acknowledgment of violence against women as a human rights issue, states, "The home is the most dangerous place for women. It often becomes a place of abuse and torture. Sexual discrimination is killing women day by day."

Spousal abuse is rampant in the United States also. The primary cause of women's injuries is their husbands' violence. Statistics show that 90 per cent of the murders of women are committed by men, and half of these men are either husbands or boyfriends. Therefore women have declared that "violence is the means used to control women's sexuality" and have made violence against women an issue since the era of the women's liberation movement in the latter half of the 1960s. However, the issue of violence against women was not given sufficient attention, either during the UN Decade for Women (1976–85) or in the Convention on the Eradication of All Discrimination against Women, known as the most important policy statement produced during this decade. Realizing this, women in the USA and in Europe began to highlight the issue of violence against women worldwide after the Third UN World Conference on Women held in Nairobi in 1985, the final year of the UN Decade for Women.

Violence against women has also emerged as the major issue of the women's movements in countries of the South. Indian women have organized nationwide in the struggle against dowry murder and rape. Violence attacks women throughout the world, especially claiming as victims women in poor countries, who are in even more disadvantaged positions.

Violence against women has become a common issue for women in countries both in the North and in the South. A worldwide campaign to collect signatures affirming that "Women's rights are human rights" was launched in anticipation of the World Conference on Human Rights, held in Vienna in 1993. As a result, the Vienna Declaration clearly defines the human rights of women and calls on all countries to expand their efforts to eradicate violence against women.

Building on the Vienna Declaration, which was achieved by the efforts of activists throughout the world, the Declaration on the Eradication of Violence against Women was adopted at the UN General Assembly at the end of 1993. The declaration classifies violence against women into three categories – domestic violence, social violence and state violence – and mandates that states shall bear the responsibility for prosecuting perpetrators and supporting victims.

In addition, the Platform for Action, adopted at the Fourth UN World Conference on Women in 1995, also includes violence against women as the fourth area of twelve critical areas of concern. It defines domestic violence, rape, sexual harassment, trafficking in women, sex tours and pornography as violations of women's human rights, and delineates strategies for their prevention. The platform also points out that empowerment rather than protection of woman victims should be the priority, together with educational training for police officers and government employees. The fifth area of concern listed in the Platform, women and armed conflict, declares rape during an armed conflict to be a war crime, and demands that strict measures be taken regarding military sexual slavery – such as the maintenance of "comfort women" – including compensation for victims and punishment of perpetrators. Many of these strategies can also be used by Japanese women.

During the first decade of the twenty-year period after the First UN World Conference on Women, held in Mexico City in 1975, the focus was on the change in gender roles and the eradication of discrimination against women. The latter half of this period focused on women's human rights, with gender violence being addressed. In most countries, husbands battering their wives has been viewed as the norm; although husbands are charged with inflicting bodily injury if they abuse women other than their wives, wife abuse has been tolerated because it is viewed as a private, domestic matter. As women, we defined such violence as a human rights violation and raised it from the level of a personal matter to a social issue for which the state should bear responsibility. It is women's power that has created the groundswell of action on the critical issue of violence against women.

Nevertheless, the development of an international standard regarding violence against women is merely the starting point in constructing a violence-free society. Women's struggle to eradicate violence will be carried over into the twenty-first century.

Part II

Women Fight the Development Invasion

A Sarawak woman proudly shows her garden

Chapter 6

The Philippines Development Plan: Forced Eviction of People and Communities

Telma's Tears

The Santa Clara Town Hall is a matchbox-like temporary hut, located about a hundred kilometres south of Manila, close to Batangas port. Waiting for us was a strong middle-aged woman, Telma Maranan, 45, Mayor of Santa Clara. We were there as one stop on the Women's Study Tour, organized by the Asia–Japan Women's Resource Centre in April 1996. The town hall was not large enough to accommodate the twenty-one members of the tour, who ranged from high-school students to retired women. Therefore we talked with Telma in an open space behind the town hall.

She told us, "We are forced to locate in temporary housing in a miserable place like this." Huts which had been put up in a haphazard way amidst foul odours from muddy roads, rotting garbage and sewage drains were home to the thin children with beautiful smiles that we saw there. For two years, Mayor Telma has lived in this environment, in a tiny "house" which barely has room enough for the three family members to lie down. Courageous Telma said in a tearful voice,

> My family had lived in Santa Clara since my grandparents' era. I was born and raised in a two-story house near the port. However, our house was demolished to expand the Batangas port. My father died over the shock of losing all he had built by his hard work. Now we are living this miserable life as displaced persons.

The Batangas Port Development Project is a part of the Calabaluzon Development Plan, the main project of the Philippines 2000

Development Plan, the symbol of the Ramos administration's strategy to make the Philippines one of the Newly Industrialized
Countries (NICs). The objective of this plan is to construct a mega-
industrial area in five states of the southern part of Luzon Island
near Manila. The master plan was developed by the Japan International Cooperation Agency (JICA). To provide a base for importing
raw materials and exporting finished products for foreign companies setting up in this area, the local Batangas port will be transformed into an international trading port as large as Manila port.
Japan's Overseas Economic Cooperation Fund (OECF) has granted a
loan of almost 6 billion yen (US$45 million) for this project. Telma
continues,

> We residents of Santa Clara did not know about this project until
> around 1990. We organized the People's Coalition Against Displace-
> ment (PCAD), to oppose the forced eviction of residents. When they
> came to evict residents, we built a human barricade to stop them.

Immediately after this Telma, the leader of this struggle, was elected
mayor in 1994, the eviction of Santa Clara residents was carried out
by force, and 1,568 families lost their homes. Telma said,

> It was just like a battlefield. Hundreds of armed police and members
> of the group assigned to carry out the eviction entered town and
> began to destroy houses, one after another. One resident was shot and
> wounded. Children and old people suffering from tear-gas bombs
> were taken to the hospital, and two of them died from heart attacks.
> Food was provided those who had suddenly lost their homes for only
> three days. What should I have done? Feeling my responsibility as
> mayor, I was almost beside myself.

Telma lit a cigarette, murmuring, "Whenever I become nervous, I
always want to smoke." She continued describing the nightmare
that took place two years earlier, saying, "We were deserted in the
heavy rain and mud and treated not as human beings, but as though
we were worn-out rags or garbage." It is said that this was the first
bloody incident related to Japan's ODA project.

Residents of Santa Clara received 35,000 pesos (US$800) in
compensation, and some moved to the new area provided by the
government eight kilometres away. However, Telma and some other
families, now about 420 in number, refused to move and instead
built shacks on vacant land close to the port, where they started life

anew. The men work as labourers on the port construction and the women work as street vendors to support themselves, but life is not easy. Telma continues,

> A very sad thing happened three days ago. We had a funeral for a 9-year-old boy who went down to the port to fish, fell into the sea and drowned. His father is a port construction worker and, because his income is unstable, his mother was forced to leave the children at home and work as a laundrywoman. The boy probably thought he could help his family by catching even a single fish. He, too, became a victim of the unstable life we have suffered since we were forcibly evicted. When will this miserable life ever end?

Once again, Telma's eyes filled with tears.

Constructing a New Town

However, Telma and her colleagues did not give in to the unfair treatment. The Japanese government, which had temporarily frozen financing for the OECF loan after the bloody eviction by force, decided to resume financing at the end of 1994, and the construction of the port started in 1995. Telma and her colleagues have given up hope of returning to their former homes, and the owner of the land they are presently occupying illegally has demanded that they leave, so they have no way of knowing when they will once again be forcibly evicted. But the residents who depend on the port for their livelihood cannot accept relocation to the distant location provided by the government. Therefore Telma and her colleagues decided to save the compensation money paid them by the government in order to buy three hectares of vacant land located near their present residence and build a new town. They changed the name of their movement to the People's Coalition for Alternative Development (the acronym remains PCAD), changing the focus of their movement from resistance to construction.

Telma went to Japan in October 1995, when Japanese citizens established the Batangas Support Fund in order to provide the needed funds for the land purchase. She appealed on behalf of the 420 families, stating,

> The development of Batangas port benefits the multinational corporations, including Japanese businesses. That is why the Japanese

government provides ODA for this project. Japanese citizens, it is your government which is destroying our livelihood and violating our human rights! Because your taxes are used for this project, you taxpayers also bear responsibility for the reality. Please stop such loans! Please support the reconstruction of our destroyed lives!

Her appeal included the words "the second Japanese invasion". Batangas port was used as a Japanese naval base during World War II, at which time some 300 Filipino homes were burned in order to construct the base, according to Telma. Approaching Batangas from Manila, one passes the town of Lipa. This area has a tragic history, long kept secret, known as the "Lipa Massacre". Thousands of local citizens were massacred by the Japanese military in their campaign to mop up anti-Japanese guerrilla resistance.

When we visited Telma, she posed the severe question:

Whom will the Batangas development benefit? It is a development invasion that sacrifices local residents' livelihood for foreign business profits without even consulting those residents. In the past, Japan carried out a military invasion. Today, it is engaging in a development invasion. When I went to Japan, I was so surprised to see how hard Japanese work! Please make an effort to learn how your hard-earned tax money is being used and how your taxes affect our lives!

The very active women who are working with Telma to construct a new community shared their thoughts at a party that night. Jugenia, aged 50, who recently became chairperson of PCAD, is raising five children and is a leader of the Batangas Port Livelihood Co-op, is a short woman overflowing with energy. She said, "My husband was a port worker and I was a street vendor. We lived a peaceful and simple family life, but everything we had was destroyed. My husband has been ill recently, and I am running a small shop to support our family. It is very painful for me that I cannot even afford my daughter's school fees so that she can go to school."

The former site of the Santa Clara community is now a vacant lot, where security guards shouldering guns stand watch at the gate. A Korean company already has begun construction inside. Sally, 27, points out a tree in the area, saying, "My house used to stand right next to that tree." At the party that night, Sally said, "Whenever I see that tree, I recall the happy life my family had and I feel sad", and she started to cry. "I watch the process of construction everyday, and I feel angry at Japan, the country that financed the development project. I want the Japanese to understand how painful it is to have our home destroyed and our town wiped out." Sally became so angry that she devoted her entire life to the opposition movement, and her husband left her. She is now raising her children single-handedly and working hard as Telma's assistant, organizing young people.

At the close of our meeting, Telma said, "Our young women are strong, so I feel hopeful about the future of Santa Clara. We will continue our struggle. Please join us."

A Letter from Mindanao

I visited Mindanao island in the southern part of the Philippines in February 1993, after receiving a letter from a Japanese woman volunteer there. The letter said,

> My friends Loloi and Dodon were killed. The photographs of their bodies show graphic evidence of torture, including over 20 stab wounds. The two were working to improve the subsistence level of small-scale, poverty-stricken fishing people who make up 80 per cent of the total number of Filipinos engaged in the fishing industry. I met Loloi for the first time last year, when I learned about the connection between Japan and the problems of Filipino fisherfolk. This was one of the reasons why I decided to return to Mindanao. He never surrendered to repeated torture and being shadowed, but continued to stand on the side of the poorest fisherfolk. Many of the fisher people in Mindanao shed tears at his death.

Both Loloi and Dodon were only 36 years old. It is thought that they were killed because they were considered problematic activists by the local government. The Japanese woman volunteer's letter issued a calm appeal, "It is Japan which has made the Filipino fisherfolk so poor. Please return what you have taken from the Philippines."

What I saw from the aeroplane heading for General Santos, a fishing port town in the southern part of Mindanao island, was mountains laid bare. Mindanao island, the second largest island in the Philippines, used to be called the Land of Promise, being blessed with rich mineral and water resources, and covered with rainforest.

The denuded mountains bear the scars of Japan's massive deforesta-tion and exportation of Philippine lauan, which has continued since the 1960s.

The General Santos airport is located in a quiet area where cows graze beside the runway and ox-carts pass by along the gravel road leading to the downtown area. Aga, a local social worker who came to the airport to meet me, wore a Malay-style dress and her head was covered with a veil. The southern part of Mindanao island is where the Muslims known as the Moros live. At the entrance of the town was displayed a huge billboard for Dole, the American agri-business, demonstrating that this is a Dole town.

The town's Lion Beach serves as a busy fishing port, with small fishing boats, called banka, moving in and out of the port. Aga pointed to a huge pile of tuna, saying, "Everyday, some ten tonnes of tuna are hauled to Davao by truck, and from there are exported to Japan by air. The first-class tuna is sent to Japan, the second-class is canned, and the poorest class is sold in the local markets." This far-away town has never been heard of in Japan; nevertheless, there is a strong connection with Japan.

As I went around the Salangani bay in a small boat, I saw the area where the mangrove forests had been cut down to make room for the shrimp-cultivation farms, which extended as far as the eye could see. I learned that the shrimp-cultivation farms cover approxi-mately 1,000 hectares, including Dole's 350-hectare farm, one of the largest in the world. When we landed, I saw the white lime powder that is used as a disinfectant blowing in the air over the drained cultivation ponds. The waste water that is drained from these ponds pollutes the ocean.

The moment I aimed my camera at the ponds, a security guard ran toward me, ordering me to hand over the film. I explained to the manager, whom the security guard had called, when he came up to see what was going on, "I am a Japanese, and when I heard that these shrimp will be exported to Japan, I just wanted to see where they are grown." Listening to my explanation, the manager changed his attitude to display warm Filipino hospitality, saying, "I am going home for lunch now. Come with me. I will treat you to a shrimp feast!" The mid-level company manager spoke as he sat in front of a dish piled high with pink boiled shrimp. "We export our shrimp to countries throughout the world, but over 80 per cent are exported to Japan. We also export tuna, octopus and squid. Japan is one of our best customers!"

Feeding Japan

Leaving the town of General Santos, I took a jeepney (a small truck used for public transportation) and headed southwest on a road that ran along the bay. All of the houses in the villages we drove through were small, hastily constructed shacks.

> Mindanao is a rich island, the home of the Muslim Moro and the tribal people. Although we resisted Spanish colonialism for three hundred years, we finally lost the land we had inherited from our ancestors at the end of the nineteenth century when the USA colonized the Philippines, and Filipino Christians, the majority people, moved in to Mindanao from other islands such as Luzon and took over our land. Furthermore, the US government mandated that all land ownership be officially registered. Those who continued living on the land registered in the name of the newly arrived Christians are regarded as illegally occupying the land. Recently, many of us have been driven off our land because of the plans for the development project.

Aga shared this story of the hardships suffered by the Moro people who comprise 25 per cent and the indigenous people who comprise 15 per cent of the 18 million residents of Mindanao island.

Finally, we reached Camba town, where we found the streets lined with elegant Spanish-style houses, in which live the owners of the land we had passed. A Japanese sea food company's fish cultivation pond was located in a coastal suburb of the town. There, terapia, a fish that resembles sea bream, is cultivated for sashimi (raw fish), frozen and exported to Japan. The Japanese manager, who quit his previous company to set up this operation, told us enthusiastically, "There's no better place to live! I only have to pay my workers 100 pesos per day, which is one-twentieth of an equivalent wage in Japan. I've already started cultivation, and I am aiming at producing a thousand tonnes per year."

But the reality is that in order to build this fish cultivation pond, twenty-one Moro families who had lived peacefully, making their living by fishing, were driven off their land. Deserted houses along the seashore and a small decaying mosque represent all that remains

Japal (right) talks about her hardship at the village to which she was forced to move

of the vanished village. I saw several simple houses built among the palm trees in the nearby village to which the villagers had moved, and the figures of women and children. Damrag Japal, 39, the village leader, said,

> A company employee suddenly appeared in our village one day and requested us to evacuate the village as his company would start fish cultivation there. He promised jobs and compensation to us, which would benefit our village, if we would leave. Although we refused, and tried our best to persist in staying there, our land had already been sold to the company. Then, the bulldozers came. Although our entire village resisted the construction, the military came in and finally drove us from the village

This means that the landowners living in the town, a national assembly member and the General Santos mayor, had sold the land, on which the villagers had lived without legal title, to a Japanese fish-cultivation company.

As I listened to each of the mothers complain about her hard life in the new village, I couldn't help but think about the relationship between this far-off coastal village in Mindanao and the dinner tables in Japan. The women in the village have never given up but continue to act, working to possess even one hectare of the land on which the twenty-one dispossessed families are currently living. Japal spoke decisively, "We women are holding meetings to appeal to the local government. We have resolved to continue our struggle until we gain the right of possession to this land. We absolutely refuse to evacuate this village!" Japal participated in the Moro liberation movement when she was young, and now she is making efforts to organize the village women. In every single word she spoke as a mother raising six children and fighting to win the village struggle, I felt Japal's strong determination to overcome any hardship and help the villagers create a new future for the village.

Port Construction for Whom?

Tamblar villlage, the community from which fishing families were about to be evicted to construct the ODA-funded fishing port, is located about thirteen kilometres southwest of General Santos. A large billboard by the side of the road read, "Proposed Construction Site of the General Santos Agri-products Processing Centre, Southern Cotabato Development Plan of the Philippine Aid Program, Funded by USAID and OECF (Japan Economic Cooperation Fund)".

Passing the inspection point at the entrance, I entered the barbed-wire enclosure, and came to a spring gushing out of the ground in the midst of a coconut palm grove, beyond which I caught a glimpse of the sparkling sea. Approaching the white sandy beach, I saw several small boats floating near the shore and naked children playing in the water.

Twenty-two Moro fishing families were living in this peaceful, beautiful seaside village. However, this village was about to be destroyed because it occupies the proposed construction site of a thousand-hectare fishing port funded by foreign aid, including Japanese ODA. Ramba Abbakal, returning from fishing, said angrily,

Although we have lived and fished here since the 1970s, they suddenly put up barbed wire two years ago, telling us to leave because they were going to build a fishing port. They declared that this land had already been sold, that they were not able to pay us any compensation, and they ordered us to move to another place. But how can

Tamblar village was wiped out in 1994, a year after my visit

we fish in a mountain area two or three hours' walk from the sea?
Although I do not want to move, I am very much afraid that the
bulldozers will come to destroy my house.

Mothers holding children gathered around us and said angrily, "It's
so unfair to drive us out without even consulting us, the residents.
The ones who will gain something from the construction of the
fishing port are the large ship owners. We want ODA stopped!"
    The village was totally destroyed the following year, in 1994.
Seeing the photographs of the sandy beach on which there was
nothing left but scrap lumber, I felt sad, knowing I could never again
hear the sounds of the palm leaves in the wind, the waves and the
innocent voices of children. Where did all the fishing families go?
Their question, "Development for whom?", still rings in my ears.

The Philippines 2000 Development Plan

I listened to the viewpoint of the Philippine government, presented
by a member of staff at the local office of the Philippine Aid Plan
(PAP). PAP bears responsibility for the South Cotabato Development

Plan, which includes the construction of this fishing port. He spread out a large map as he explained,

> This is a development plan of ODAs from the USA, Japan, Germany and Italy, to promote agricultural- and marine-products processing in this area, improve transportation and promote exportation through the construction of an international airport, a modern port, highways, telephone communication system, an agricultural- and marine-products processing centre and hydraulic power.

The destinations of marine products such as shrimp and tuna, and agricultural products including pineapples, bananas and vegetables were indicated by arrows on the map. The largest number of arrows pointed to Japan.

The official stressed that "this development plan will benefit no country more than Japan, the largest importer of Filipino agricultural and marine products. When both the port and the international airport are completed, we can export fresher and larger amounts of tuna to Japan than we do now." This statement clearly reveals the reason why Japan is cooperating by providing ODA funding for the South Cotabato Development Plan. It is to serve Japanese corporate and consumer interests, and the end result is that Tamblai village was destroyed.

The fishing people's question, "Development for whom?", is directed at the Philippines 2000 Development Plan of the Ramos administration's large-scale development plan, which is funded by foreign capital and aid. It includes the South Cotabato Development Plan; the Calabaluzon Development Plan in the Manila area, including the enlargement of Batangas port; the Kagayan de Oro Development Plan; and the Samar Island Development Plan in northern Mindanao. These plans have led to the forcible eviction of local residents from their communities and the sacrifice of poverty-stricken individuals.

Not only marine products but also everything from lumber to fruit and vegetables is being exported from South Cotabato to Japan. Heading inland from General Santos, we passed Poromolock, another Dole town. Vast pineapple plantations stretched over 12,000 hectares, further than the human eye can see. A Dole staff member said, "The largest amount of pineapple is exported to Japan in canned form." Again, I discovered a connection between this area and Japan.

A leader of the 4,200-member plantation labour union expressed concern about workers' health problems, saying,

> For the workers, the problems resulting from the use of agricultural chemicals are very serious. Although it is dangerous for farm workers to enter the area where the agricultural chemicals have been spread until five days after crop-dusting, we are forced to return to work immediately. Many workers complain of health problems such as skin disease and lung disorders. Because we have so many women workers, we are seriously concerned about the effects of agricultural chemicals in terms of their reproductive health.

However, for fear of losing their jobs, the workers cannot appeal to the management to stop using agricultural chemicals.

Vast fields of asparagus could be seen around the edges of the plantation. This is also a Dole project in which about six hundred farm households cultivate asparagus for export to Japan. We visited one farm where the farmer told us,

> We used to plant corn, but since Dole offers financing, about two years ago we signed a contract to plant two hectares of asparagus. But Dole buys only the products that pass inspection for exportation, paying a mere 32 pesos [70¢] per kilogramme, so it takes many years to pay off our loans.

He told us that only about 35 per cent of his products pass inspection for exportation, and the rest are sold in the local markets at even cheaper prices. I looked at the mountain of green asparagus, realizing that only the very top quality ever reaches Japanese dinner tables. On our way home, as we drove along the farm road passing between the fields of asparagus plants, the leaves of which were rustling in the wind, the farm woman who accompanied me said,

> I also once worked on an asparagus farm as a day labourer. But I only earned 40 pesos per day, which didn't even cover transportation costs, so I quit. I know that asparagus farmers cannot pay any more than that, because they have to repay the money they borrowed from Dole or they will lose their land.

Beyond the asparagus fields, Dole was beginning to produce decorative plants such as anthurium for use in flower arrangements in Japan.

Once again, I witnessed North–South issues at work here: on the one hand, American agribusiness and Japanese consumers; on the other hand, local farmers and women workers.

The Violence of Economic Development

Near the Japanese fish-cultivation ponds stood a lumber factory. Lauan logs one metre in diameter were piled mountain-high everywhere. Peering into the lumber factory between the mountains of logs, I could see the name of a lumber company in Osaka, Japan. Aga said, "Almost all the forests in Mindanao have been stripped bare. Japanese businesses are carrying off all the forests around the town of Camba, even those that have escaped destruction until now." From the seashore, I could see that a boat which was used to transport lumber bore a Japanese name. Standing on the spot where Japan was about to plunder even the last forest of Mindanao, I keenly sensed the violence of Japanese economic development.

All the harvest of the ocean, the mountains, the fields and the forests is taken for the use of the affluent society, the satiated society – Japan. As a consequence, the impoverished people in the society that originally possessed these resources are made even poorer. Aga talked about the extent of the Moro fishing people's poverty,

> Eighty per cent of the people in South Cotabato are as poor as
> Filipinos in other areas, living at poverty level and not even having
> enough to eat. Although many of the Moro people make their living
> by fishing, they cannot catch as many fish as before. Even by fishing
> all day long, they can only earn 25 pesos, and some days, they can
> only afford one meal.

Because of the over-fishing by large commercial fishing boats, water pollution from the waste emitted by shrimp-cultivation farms, and soil erosion resulting from deforestation, the fishing catch has decreased. Consequently, thirty thousand subsistence fisherfolk and their families have been driven to the depths of poverty. In one tragic case, a fisherman became neurotic due to lack of food, killing one after another his six children who cried from hunger at night. No one was able to calm him, and finally they had to shoot the father.

I also learned of the indigenous people who were driven into extreme poverty. I visited one village of the Rumad tribe, located on a slope overlooking the ocean. Thirty families, about two hundred people, were living in simple houses built high off the ground. Women in hand-woven traditional clothing appeared and spoke one by one, saying, "We are growing corns and cassava, but recently, because the forests have been destroyed, we cannot get food and our lives have become very difficult. We cannot even send our children to school." Aga, who formerly was involved in activities in this village, said,

> The Rumad, a mountain people, are desperately poor. Recently, sixty-two children died of measles over a two-month period in a mountain village sixty kilometres from here. This happened because they suffered from malnutrition and also because they were not able to receive any medical care.

In order to escape from poverty and improve their lives, Rumad women work in Middle Eastern countries that have the same Islamic tradition. Aga, who had helped organize the Moro Women's Association, said with regret,

> We managed to organize the Moro Women's Association in the 1980s and about a thousand women became members. But the number has decreased to half due to the increase of migrant workers who went abroad to work. One hundred out of the five hundred women migrant workers escaped their situation and returned home after experiencing sexual violence or nonpayment of wages. One woman was even killed.

Thus, in this area where people are short of food and greatly troubled by having their land taken from them, one thousand hectares of coastal land is used for shrimp cultivation and tens of thousands of hectares inland are used for banana and pineapple cultivation for exportation to rich countries. For the people of Mindanao, development means having their land and food taken from them.

Those who take action to change this unfair structure and support poor fishing people will be killed by those supporting such development, just as Loloi and Dodon, who led me to Mindanao, were. Aga told me that more than twenty people close to her, including friends and colleagues, have been killed. We cannot ignore the blood and tears shed in Mindanao: the island into which huge amounts of Japanese ODA have been poured and to which many Japanese companies have flocked, in order to serve as the food-producing base for Japan and enrich Japanese dinner tables.

Chapter 7

Thai Village Women Protest Eucalyptus Plantations and Shrimp Cultivation

A Visit to Northeast Thailand

Thai village women from both agricultural and fishing communities brought the scent of the soil and the sea to the Asian Women's Workshop on Alternatives in Action at the NGO Forum of the Beijing Fourth UN World Conference on Women. They spoke powerfully about their experience of resisting the loss of their farmland and fishing sites due to rapid economic growth. Their speeches were filled with criticism of Japan. Through this workshop, I learned what had happened in the remote villages in northeast Thailand and the distant seaside fishing villages in southern Thailand, and about the relationship between Japan and these villages. I felt that I must see it with my own eyes, and so I visited them in February 1996.

The northeast district, Isan, is the poorest region in Thailand. Fong, a woman staff member of a northeast Thai agricultural village development NGO in Khonkaen, and I drove over the parched land on a dusty road in her jeep. This area used to be covered with a thick forest, but now the forest is gone, leaving only the desolate landscape that stretched out before us.

It was evening when we reached Ing's village, located in Royet Province, in southern Isan. Ing, 42, was the woman who appealed "Stop Eucalyptus Forestation" most vocally at the Beijing workshop. She invited me into her typical Thai farmhouse, built high off the ground. Her sunburned face broke into a pleased smile at our first meeting since the Beijing conference. She said, "We are going to have a villagers' meeting here tonight. We are going to take our

Ing, a village leader, in pious Buddhist prayer at the village temple

protest to the provincial office next week, so we plan to discuss that
issue tonight." Her facial expression changed from that of an ordinary
farm woman to that of a leader in the village struggle.

I was treated to the special dinner of sticky rice, vegetables and
chicken that is unique to Isan. After dinner, villagers appeared one
by one, gathering in the yard in front of Ing's house. More than a
hundred people sat crowded together, their legs tucked under them,
on the woven mat spread on the ground. I saw the faces of men and
women, old people and children, lit by the dim electric light. After
the meeting opened with Ing's greeting, people stood up, one by
one, and voiced what seemed to be their individual appeals. A young
NGO worker, who had accompanied me from Bangkok, said, "Isan

dialect is difficult to translate!" Thus, she was unable to interpret for me. Finally, she did translate the explanation of a young villager who could speak the standard Thai language. I felt the great distance between Isan and Bangkok.

Ing's appeal was especially powerful. At the top of her voice, she asserted, "Let's continue to struggle together until we recover our farmland, which has been taken from us by eucalyptus forestation. We have fought for many years, so we have nothing to fear! Let's appeal to the governor to put a stop to eucalyptus forestation and return our land!" Ing made me stand and she introduced me, Japan International Cooperation Agency (JICA) supports eucalyptus forestation, since Japan buys eucalyptus trees in the form of pulp chips to make paper. Let's ask this Japanese friend, who has stood in solidarity with Thai women, to report on the Japanese situation." At the Beijing workshop, Ing had stressed to Japanese participants, "We want Japanese women to act with us to stop eucalyptus forestation!" To tell the truth, I didn't feel comfortable standing before the villagers who were suffering from and strongly resisting eucalyptus forestation. However, I tried to explain Japanese–Thai relations regarding eucalyptus forestation, sharing the stories I had heard from people in Thai environmental groups and the reports I had written as a journalist in Japan.

> In the 1980s, when the Thai military government enforced the eucalyptus forestation policy based on the Isan greening project, Japan supported it through technical cooperation. JICA built four seedbed centres in Isan, and sent experts to oversee planting. Agreement was reached on a joint company established by more than ten major Japanese paper companies, which would import the eucalyptus pulp chips made from eucalyptus trees that would reach their full growth in only four to five years. In Japan, the consumption of paper is increasing due to the custom of over-wrapping purchased items, printed advertisements, and computerization. It is said that the annual average consumption of 225 kilogrammes of paper by each Japanese is second only to the USA. Probably only about 20 kilogrammes, one-twentieth of that consumed by the Japanese, is consumed per person per year in Thailand.

I pulled out of my pocket a packet of tissues and showed it to the villagers. It was one of the packets of tissues handed out freely at train stations in Japan to advertise products or services. This created a stir among the villagers, who were listening to me intently. I found myself unable to say that these tissue packets were often used to advertise the sex industry and loan agencies. I said, "I will carry back to Japan the story of your struggle and try to convince the Japanese not to waste paper."

Finally, I told them about the situation of over ten thousand young Thai women who are being sold and sent to Japan by trafficking syndicates each year, where they are forced to work in Japan's sex industry as sex slaves. I warned the villagers, "Please be careful not to let your daughters experience such a tragedy." My words created a commotion. They told me that young women from a nearby village are working in Japan. When I visited another Isan village during my trip, a mother asked me to give a dress she had made from hand-woven cloth and a letter to her daughter, who had gone to Japan to work. The mother said that the name and address of the Japanese man on the letter was that of the husband of the daughter's Thai woman boss. It reminded me of the Shimodate case in which three Thai women murdered their Thai woman boss. I wondered whether the mother really knew her daughter's situation, and was concerned.

Confrontation with the Military

The next morning, I was riding along a dusty road on a tractor headed toward the eucalyptus plantation with Ing and several other village women. I heard that a policeman who had been at the meeting the previous night had asked about me. This morning, that same policeman was following us, accompanied by another police-man on a motorbike. Ing was not worried about policemen, saying, "Policemen are always following us, so I am used to it." She con-tinued, "We tried to protect our land every way we could. We held sit-ins on the planned site of the plantation project to resist, but we were forcibly removed by weapons-bearing military personnel and policemen. Women have always stood on the front line in order to prevent bloodshed, even at the risk of our lives." Seated atop the strongly vibrating tractor, Ing began to tell the story of her ten-year struggle against eucalyptus forestation.

Going two or three kilometres beyond the cluster of village houses, we reached a vast expanse of eucalyptus forest that seemed

The vast expanse of eucalyptus plantation, in which not a blade
of grass can grow

to extend endlessly. Not a single blade of grass grew on the parched
land. The slim, deadly white trunks of the eucalyptus trees stretched
up to the sky everywhere. What a contrast to the green rainforest
with its myriad varieties of trees. If rainforests appear to be a world
of life, eucalyptus forests appear to be a world of death. Eucalyptus
trees grow so quickly that they absorb all the water and nutrients
from the soil, making it impossible for other plants to grow in the
same forest; thus they are given the name "gang trees". Ing cursed
the trees, saying, "I want to cut them all down." She continued to
talk about the history of the women's struggle:

> In 1985, the government declared the land we had always farmed to
> be a national protected forest area and sold it to a private company.
> The company planted eucalyptus trees and the eucalyptus forestation
> began. We burned the young plants, because we did not want them
> to grow. Then the police came and the conflict began. The policemen
> burned down eleven houses and arrested twenty-one villagers. Out of
> this experience, we realized that women have to be on the front line

in order to save a difficult situation through peaceful negotiations, because when men confront the government authorities, violence breaks out.

Ing said that she would never forget the first time she went to the provincial government office with some five hundred villagers in 1989. She said with regret,

> I can only speak our dialect. I was not able to understand what the government officials were saying. I was so nervous that I was per-spiring even though the government office was air-conditioned. They treated us as country bumpkins who could not speak the language spoken in Bangkok. But our situation is so serious that we decided to go to Bangkok and appeal directly to the prime minister. We had neither money nor food, but we just got on a bus bound for Bang-kok. We were told to go to the Ministry of Agriculture, so we went there and conducted a sit-in demonstration.

However, the government responded by sending military forces to Ing's village. Ing and her colleagues returned to their village and conducted a sit-in in the forest to confront the military. Ing said, "We made every effort to avoid bloodshed. Wherever I went, even to the fields, I was followed and watched by the soldiers, but, unafraid, I often went to the government offices to issue our peti-tion and negotiate."

"Reduce Paper Consumption!"

Ing and her colleagues were not able to triumph over the power of military force. "The military were always stationed here, and under military protection the company proceeded with its forestation project by the use of force." We arrived at the water's edge in a place like a park in the eucalyptus plantation. Over ten cows with bells around their necks were chewing the cud at the water's edge. Ing pointed out an elderly farmer, saying,

> He also had his land taken way and so was not able to engage in farming. Since then, he has become a cattle herder.
>   There was one person who was arrested and fined 100,000 bahts [US$2,500] for cutting down eucalyptus trees planted on his own land. He had no other alternative except to sell his house and leave the village. We could do nothing to help him. I wonder where he is and what he is doing now.

Usually fearless, Ing's face became gloomy. On our way home, Ing pointed to an area, saying, "My farmland was around there. We will never give up! We will continue our struggle until we recover our land!" Listening to Ing's words, the women accompanying us raised their clenched fists.

I had thought that the eucalyptus plantation project had been suspended after the military administration was toppled by the Thai democratization movement in 1992. However, Fong, my guide, said, "The eucalyptus plantation continues throughout Isan, as the officials employed many underhanded means, including bribing influential village men and taking advantage of the weak position of villagers who have no legal title to their land."

We headed for the northern part of Isan. At Sakonakhon, a town located in the central part of northern Isan, we saw some three hundred farmers assembled at an old temple. They had come together to make preparations to visit the provincial governor to carry on negotiations the following week. The participants were fiercely criticizing the local province forestry officials and the national park officials in front of a large golden statue of Buddha.

> Why don't they return our land? They told us we must vacate our land in order to protect the national parks, but the trees and all living things are already gone. We farmed there for many generations. It is terrible of them to drive us away now. Let them arrest us if they so desire! There will be food to eat in the police station detention centre.

When Moi, 41, a woman leader in the textile-weaving village close to Sakonakhon, spoke out clearly, the women assembled at the meeting, old and young alike, applauded enthusiastically. A very thin 71-year-old woman, who was eating sticky rice and other food out of a round basket as she listened to the speech, said, "I had the land which I had worked for a long time taken away, so I always participate in all the demonstrations. I am not afraid of death! I am going to participate in the demonstration at the provincial government office next week."

After the meeting, I stayed overnight in Moi's village. The next morning, I was given a send-off with the traditional Bashi ritual. Village women had made a beautiful decoration of banana leaves and wild flowers which they had gathered. They tied around my wrist cotton threads called bashi, as a prayer for my safe journey.

Their parting gift was a colourful, hand-woven cotton cloth. They said, "Please use this cloth in place of tissue or paper." I received it as their message to all Japanese people: "Please reduce paper consumption!"

The anti-eucalyptus-plantation struggle has spread throughout Isan. How many village people have been thrown into great distress by Thailand's rapid economic development? Many stories of villagers' protests against eucalyptus forestation are told in the book *Behind a Smile: Voices of Thailand*, written with empathy by Sanitsuda Ekachai, a *Bangkok Post* woman journalist who had travelled to local villages to listen to the villagers' stories.

One such story describes the 130 families who were forced to move to a protected forest area in Donyai, where they were made to cooperate with the government's anti-Communist guerrilla purge in the 1970s. In the 1980s, these families were forced to move again to make way for the eucalyptus plantation project. The villagers resisted by cutting down young eucalyptus trees and seizing the bulldozers. Finally, however, their orchards and tapioca fields were destroyed. The village women, protecting a single jackfruit tree with all their might, questioned, "If the government allows us to grow fruit and rubber, we can supply both the green vegetation promoted by the nation and the food that human beings require. Why can't poor farmers like us produce the food we need?"

The government does not allow farmers to plant trees appropriate to the area in order to restore the forests so that food such as fruit and mushrooms can be produced. The government even sends military forces in to take over the farmland, orchards and grazing land, and drive farmers out. Isn't the real purpose of the eucalyptus plantation programme of the Thai government the accumulation of foreign currency by promoting exportation to foreign countries like Japan, rather than tree planting for the restoration of the forests? Aren't Thai and Japanese companies and the Japanese consumers the ones who really profit?

When I returned to Khonkaen, the starting point of my travels in Isan, a staff member of the Northeast Agricultural Village Development NGO committee showed me a map of Isan, explaining in great detail,

> Farmers are losing their land not only due to eucalyptus forestation
> but also because of other waves of development projects flooding into

Isan. There are plans to construct over forty dams on three rivers; twelve have already been constructed, driving farmers off their land in the process. Pollution results from the construction of paper-pulp and electronics factories. In addition, golf courses and tourist resorts are being developed. The Japanese government has shown interest in the Isan Area Development Plan, sending investigation teams and opening a JICA office in Khonkaen to promote technical cooperation.

He issued a strong appeal to Japan, saying,

> The problem is international cooperation for the development plan that threatens local residents' lives without even consulting their opinions. Japanese citizens must monitor JICA activities to a greater extent.

A Fishing Village in the South

The village of 31-year-old Miya — who had issued a strong appeal at a workshop at the Beijing Conference NGO Forum, saying, "Our lives are endangered by shrimp cultivation. Don't eat shrimp" — was located along the seashore on the outskirts of Trang Province close to the Malaysian border. Southern Thailand, with its vivid green foliage, forms a stark contrast to the northeast area, where the natural environment has been destroyed. However, fishing folk's lives are poor. Miya's village is located at the foot of steep cliffs. The village has neither electricity nor running water, and the houses are like shanties. Miya tells us,

> Since Japanese and other large foreign trawling boats have come, our catch of fish has decreased. In addition, as shrimp cultivation spreads, mangroves are cut down, contaminated waste water pollutes the sea, making our catch even less. We have only a small fishing boat, so we can do nothing to compensate for the decrease. Some people migrate to the city to work because they cannot support themselves here.

Miya's husband is a fisherman, and the couple have six children to support. Because she is a village health worker, she is deeply concerned about the difficulties the village endures.

> Just when we were at a complete loss, a staff member from the environmental protection NGO Yadofon [raindrops] Foundation in Trang came to our village, and taught us that fish and other marine life would return if we protected and restored the deteriorating environment of the sea. We learned that water grasses are especially

Miya with her husband; she said "I want to protect the sea"

essential to hatching fish eggs, and so we started a movement to
protect them. As a result, the dugong, which had disappeared from
the sea for 10 years, has returned. It's a precious mammal in our sea.

Miya told her story with pleasure as we sat in a bamboo meeting
place built by the villagers. It may just be the mannerisms of the
southern Thai people, but Miya seemed to be a very calm, happy
woman.

We went down to the seashore, where I saw several small fishing
boats bobbing up and down on the waves. I was captivated by the
quiet and the beauty of the scene before me. Miya said, "We have
to prevent the sea from being taken away from us by the tourist
companies." Every word of this fishing woman, dressed in a simple

cotton wraparound skirt, communicated her strong determination to protect her village. "We have also learned about the methods of fishing. We have ceased destructive means, for example, dynamite fishing, in order to protect our sea. We just want to fish near home without having to work in a factory as we did before."

The efforts of Miya and her colleagues may be the trifling attempts of small-scale fisherfolk to resist the powerful development interests that are backed by massive capital investment, whose huge trawling boats and vast areas of shrimp cultivation are about to destroy the ocean village. But I found profound meaning in and was deeply moved by Miya's strenuous efforts, hearing her declare, "We experienced family conflicts over the small amount of money we made in the city. But now, although we are poor, we want to build a community where we can live in harmony with the sea and support one another." Thus, her appeal "Don't eat too much shrimp" really hit home.

Japan consumes more than 3 kilogrammes of shrimp per person every year. As such, it is the largest shrimp-importing and consuming country in the world. In addition, Japan is the largest tuna-consuming country in the world. Japanese consumption of fish as a whole is remarkably large, nearly 80 kilogrammes per person per year, approximately three times that of Thailand, where the average is over 20 kilogrammes per person per year. Furthermore, it is not only human beings who eat fish in Japan, a country now caught up in a pet boom. Tuna, imported especially for cat food, are caught in the Philippines and in Indonesia, canned in Thailand and exported to Japan. Recently, high-quality pet food, including even shrimp, has become popular.

To supply the growing Japanese market, over-fishing has created a shortage of fish, resulting in the seashores of Asian countries being destroyed for fish cultivation. This is carried out in the same systematic way as the deforestation of natural forests and the planting of eucalyptus trees. The victims of this system are farmers who are driven off their land and fisherfolk who are being deprived of their fishing grounds. As a result of my travels in Thailand and my encounters with women who are engaged in the struggle to oppose eucalyptus forestation and shrimp cultivation, I saw clearly the relationship between the development exploiters and the exploited victims – in short, the global gap between the North and the South, and the domestic gap between cities and rural villages.

Chapter 8

Indigenous People Fight Deforestation and Dam Construction in Sarawak

Anti-logging Blockade

A four-hour flight took me to Sarawak, one of the states of Malaysia that is located in the northern section of Borneo, the island of indigenous people that is covered with thick tropical rainforests. It was ten years ago that I first went to Sarawak. My next visit was five years later; since then, the image of the indigenous women of Sarawak has remained in my heart.

Sarawak is a country of rivers, large and small, which run among green forests and function as substitute roads. I took a boat heading north on the Baram river. On the boat with me were an elderly woman, her earlobes stretched long with weights and her hands and neck tattooed following traditional custom; a young mother carrying her baby on her back in a colourful basket made of black and yellow beads; and young girls dressed in the latest style, wearing T-shirts and jeans. The variety of dress I saw on the boat clearly reveals the changes taking place in Sarawak.

It was on this river trip that I first saw a village of longhouses, unique to Sarawak. Then, a lumber camp with mountains of logs piled high came into view. Rafts of logs 100 metres in length were floating slowly down the muddy brown river. I could surmise that mass deforestation was taking place upstream.

Along the way, I changed to a small boat, known as a longboat, and continued upstream. We finally landed, after passing through many swirling rapids, and then drove about two hours by jeep over the reddish brown logging road that ran through the forest. We

The piers before longhouses are crowded with indigenous people
taking boats along the river

finally arrived after dark at a small village, having driven through
heavy rain. It was a village of the Penan people, who are known
among the more than twenty indigenous tribes in Sarawak for
retaining the original, traditional lifestyle.

This was my first visit and, to be honest, I felt very uneasy. My
guide, Thomas Jarong, a member of an environmental organization
and himself a young man from the Kenya tribal group, introduced
me to a man with short bobbed hair who stuck his head out of the
door of a wooden hut, and invited us inside. Men and women were
gathering in the dark room that was lit by one small lamp set on
the floor. One after another, they shook my hand courteously to
welcome me. The young men, who were wearing only shorts, were
strongly built with attractive features; the women, clad in batik
sarongs, were charming; and the children were lovely. More than
twenty families or some hundred villagers had gathered, filling the
meeting room.

I heard that they were the Penan nomadic tribal people who
lived in the interior of the jungle; they would quickly put up huts

of wood and banana leaves, hunt in the area, collect sago (starch made from the powder in the centre of sago palm trunks) and mushrooms, and then move on to another place after several months. I had imagined how fierce a people they must be, but, on the contrary, they seemed very calm and gentle. They warmly welcomed this Japanese woman, whom they were seeing for the first time, just as if she were one of their old friends.

Jarong explained that over half of the Sarawak trees that are felled are exported to Japan. After carrying on a heated discussion, Wan Maron, the village chief, stated, "Although we relied on the forest for our lives, logging came to this area; since then, we have not been able to make a living here. Please stop cutting down our trees. We do not want the Japanese to take our timber. We will stop logging by force."

At the beginning of 1986, when the Japanese actually built an iron bridge upstream over the Tutoh river to use in logging, the Penan villagers, including Wan Maron, held a sit-in and engaged in a blockade campaign. Although they were removed by the police after two days, their action served to inform the world of the crisis in Sarawak. Building on their experience, they planned a simultaneous blockade campaign of logging roads everywhere in Sarawak. I visited them while they were in the process of discussing this campaign.

The blockade campaign was launched in March 1987, just after my visit. Men, women and children conducted sit-ins in over ten rainforest locations where logging had already begun. Their human barricades successfully stopped logging operations for several months, during which time the amount of timber exported decreased dramatically.

Logging Road Blockade Campaigns

The forests are the source of our livelihood, provide our lives. We lived here before the outsiders came, fishing in the clear water, hunting in the jungle, cooking sago and eating fruit. Although our life was hard, we were satisfied. However, a logging company has muddied our river and destroyed our jungle. Fish cannot live in the dirty river and wild animals cannot live in the depleted forests. You are robbing us of our livelihood and threatening our very lives. We want you to return our land handed down to us by our ancestors. Stop destroying our forests. Respect our lives and culture!

The gifts of the forest are taken away due to destruction by logging

This declaration was sent to Japan through overseas support organizations and expressed the Penan people's sense of impending crisis. A Japanese-affiliated logging company was also operating in this area at the time. The fact that the Japanese government financed bridge construction for this company with ODA funds became a problem in the Japanese Diet.

After spending the night at Wan Marong's house – actually more of a hut than a house – I was able to see the Penan forest people's daily life. I saw a middle-aged couple early next morning, who were going out hunting together. The husband carried a spear, *paran* (mountain knife) and blow darts; the wife carried large woven mats and baskets. Walking along, side by side, they seemed to be very close. They complained, "Recently, even though we walk in the forest for two or three days, we sometimes are not able to bring home any game."

Going down to the riverside behind the house, I saw a young mother bathing her daughter and, beside her, a boy, catching fish in a net. What a deep silence there is in the forest! On the river bank an elderly couple were extracting starch by filtering sago. The husband, wearing a loincloth, was hitting a thick sago palm branch with his *paran* to extract the fibres inside, which he placed on the handmade mat. The wife wore bead bracelets and had her sarong hitched up around her, as she poured river water on the fibre and trod on it with both feet. What a great partnership the elderly couple had, working together in this way for many decades. After a while, they stopped their labour, and the wife pulled her sarong to one side and pointed to her stomach to show me that she was hungry. I was told that the sago palm trees have dramatically decreased as a result of logging. For the Penan, sago starch is the staple food, just like rice is for the Japanese.

The forest people cannot live if the gifts of the forests, such as sago palm trees, animals, fish and rattan, are taken from them. The Penan do not like to fight; they share everything they catch amongst themselves, even the smallest animal or fish. Yet even these peaceful people have been driven to carry on a road blockade campaign.

Frequent Logging Accidents

At the Marons' house, Wan's wife, Rango, was weaving a bead basket. Whenever we talked about her children and her family, she suddenly burst into tears. She talked about her oldest son, Agun, who had been killed in a logging accident the previous year.

> We used to be able to get all our food in the forest, but recently we have to earn money to buy food and other things we need, so Agun had to go to work for a logging company. He was in an accident while working in the interior. We were informed that he had been taken to a hospital in Marudi, and although my husband and I went downriver immediately, his body was already cold by the time we saw him. Agun was such a gentle son.

It would have been impossible for them to reach the hospital in time to prevent his death if they had had to travel on the same logging road I had first driven over to get to the river and then take a boat downriver.

In this way, many women lose their husbands, sons or brothers in logging accidents. The death rate in Sarawak due to logging accidents is twenty-one times that of similar accidents in industrialized countries such as Canada. On my way home, I visited a general hospital in Marudi town, close to the mouth of the Baram river. Christina, a staff member of the same environmental organization as my guide, Thomas Jarong, is from the Kayan tribal group. Her voice became tearful as she said,

> My nephew was killed in an accident on the logging site when he became entangled in a thick rope. He was just 20 years old at the time, and was overjoyed at being a new father. His teenage wife wept as she returned to her family home, a longhouse, carrying their baby. I wonder how they are doing now.

At the hospital in Marudi, I saw a young man, his legs wrapped in bandages, being carried in on a stretcher and a woman who appeared to be his mother at his side, murmuring words of encouragement. Moans could be heard coming out of the hospital rooms. I was told that the lower half of the body of the middle-aged man in the bed in the corner of one room had become paralysed because a large tree had toppled over on him. He had been in the hospital for many years. In the hospital yard, two or three young men with only one leg each were slowly practising how to walk again using crutches. A Malay nurse said,

> The number of surgical patients who are admitted to this ward due to logging accidents is the highest in this hospital. Including light injuries, four or five new patients enter the hospital every day. We moved a young man who had a serious head injury to the brain surgery ward at Miri. Sometimes, the bodies of people who have already died are brought to this hospital. It is so painful to see the families weeping and wailing to express their grief.

Logging accidents happen frequently because the workers, who work for low wages, are paid according to the number of trees they fell, so they have to work until it becomes pitch-dark on the steep slopes deep in the mountains, no longer on the flat plains where most of the trees have already been felled. Many workers are pinned under huge trees or their bodies are pierced by sharp branches. In addition, driving large machinery such as bulldozers on the soft red clay at the logging sites without undergoing sufficient training is also a leading cause of accidents.

Four indigenous women from Sarawak visited Japan in the spring of 1991 to deliver their earnest appeal at the Testimonies of Forest Women Meeting. They testified,

Since January of this year alone, in only four months, thirty-three of our men have died from logging accidents. We don't want to send our fathers, our husbands and our brothers to do such dangerous work! If Japanese people continue to live such wasteful life styles, it will destroy the lives of the forest people of the world. We beseech you, for the sake of our children and grandchildren, not to rob Sarawak of its forests!

Truly, the very blood of the indigenous men and the tears of the indigenous women are being shed. What sacrifices does it require to produce the timber imported from Sarawak, which is then disposed of without hesitation after being imported to Japan and used for concrete construction panels, building materials and furniture? Listening to the testimonies of these women, the pain that I had felt at the hospital returned.

Return to Sarawak

I visited Sarawak again in the spring of 1991. I was travelling with Korean and Filipino women. We took a boat up the Rajang river, the longest river in Malaysia. The man who came to meet us at the Belaga port from Longang, our final destination, was very frightened that he might be seen by the police. We set out before daybreak the next morning, going out the back door and heading for the river tributary, where we boarded a long boat in order to escape from police observation. We got off the boat and walked along the river in places where the current was too rapid. Finally, eight hours later, we reached Longang. We had heard that the Kenya tribal villagers had continued their anti-logging road blockade campaign for almost a year.

In Longang, we found 122 families living in seven longhouses. A long veranda called a *luai* served as the common space. It was used every night as a stage where villagers sing and dance, playing the three-stringed *sape*, a traditional guitar. It also served as the democratic forum where both men and women in the community assembled to discuss community issues. They told us that the decision to carry on the road blockade campaign was also made here. A man with a moustache said, "Last year a man who went out hunting in the forest found the logging road. He ran back to the village to inform everyone. Then we decided to blockade the road to resist the

Kenya tribal women in Longang talked about the blockade campaign.

logging. We will never allow any logging company to invade our land! I do not care if I am run over by a tractor while I am sitting-in in front of it." A middle-aged woman with tattoos on her hands spoke out strongly, "I'm supporting my sons in participating in the road blockade. I myself am determined to struggle in order to preserve the forest for our children!"

So, thirty to forty men set out and walked for four hours to reach the lumber site, where they blocked the road used to transport food to the logging site. However, one month later, eight people were arrested; subsequently, fourteen more were arrested. They said, "Our hands were tied behind our backs, and we were taken by boat and thrown into a lockup of the Belaga police station. They did not provide us with blankets even though it was so cold at night that we couldn't sleep!" All of them were then taken downriver by boat to Sibu, where they were imprisoned for six months. Even after that, the area was watched by security police; therefore, when we returned to Belaga by boat, we put a vinyl sheet over our heads to conceal ourselves from the eyes of the police.

Undaunted by such hardships, all of the Longang villagers continued their struggle for a year. Fearing that logging could occur while they were not looking, the men continued the road blockade twenty-four hours a day in shifts; they cooked their own food onsite. While their husbands are continuing the road blockade sit-in campaign, the women take care of their homes, care for the children and farm the fields to produce food. It is the women who bear the heavy responsibility of supporting their families while their husbands face arrest and imprisonment.

The next year, at the beginning of 1992, I received a letter from Sarawak informing me that an elderly man and a 15-year-old boy, who had been monitoring the logging road blockade site, had been arrested by fifty armed police, and the protest movement's hut had been destroyed by a bulldozer. Furthermore, all forty-two men who had gone out in search of the two who had been carried off were themselves arrested and sent to the police station in Kapit by boat.

The indigenous people throughout Sarawak, including the Penan and the Kenya, refuse to stop resisting logging even though they are arrested again and again. Although a trip on the river in the rainforest when the sun shines and the birds sing always consoles my spirit, on that same river route, the indigenous people, who have hitherto lived peacefully, are tied up with ropes and taken to the police station. They are thrown into a police detention centre, judged by the modern legal system of which they have no knowledge, and imprisoned or fined. How much do we know about their lifestyle in the longhouses in the abundantly blessed forest, their aboriginal culture and their spirit, all of which have made them struggle, even at the expense of making such a heavy sacrifice? How much are we aware of our responsibility for their suffering as a result of our consumer lifestyle?

Dams and Iban Destiny

It is not only logging that brings suffering to the indigenous people of Sarawak. Dam construction also threatens their lives. Batang Ai dam, located about three hundred kilometres southeast of Kuching, the capital of Sarawak, close to the Indonesian border in Kalimantan, was completed in 1985 by two Japanese construction companies partially funded by Japanese ODA. The dam construction resulted in

3,000 Iban people, the largest tribal group in Sarawak, who were living in twenty-one longhouses, being evicted from their homes and forced to resettle in another location. I visited their resettlement area in the spring of 1991 in order to learn how they were surviving in their drastically different living conditions, changing their traditional life of cultivating rice to slash-and-burn farming and hunting.

Although previously living in longhouses on the river banks, their new houses stood lined up like a housing subdivision, built in a hollow following deforestation of the area. On the verandas, women were drying peppers and weaving baskets. Semai, 26, a mother of four children, was holding her baby as she spoke,

> We have an agreement with the development authorities that one person from each family will be hired by the plantation. But we cannot live on the plantation wages, which are only 8 lingits (US$2) per day, and we cannot work on rainy days. My husband went to work in Bintulu a month ago.

It is impossible to live even on the maximum income of 240 lingits per month (US$63), which is still far below the poverty line in Malaysia. Over thirty men from her longhouse of thirty-six families had left home to go and work in the city and two entire families had moved to the city because of the difficulty in supporting themselves. Some men have gone abroad to work in Singapore and Taiwan, and some women have even gone to work in the sex industry in town. Semai continued, "I am growing peppers to contribute to our living expenses." She showed me the garden plot allotted to each family. "With my husband gone, I feel very lonely and worried. Some women are concerned that their husbands may become intimate with other women in the city where they are working." I sensed the concern of this young wife behind her calm smile.

Chungdai, 65, who lives next-door to Semai, tattooed from her throat to her chest, was a woman of typical Iban dignity. She said,

> Life in our former village was good. We lived simply, but we never had to worry about money. Although my son works on the plantation, fulfilling the agreement to hire one person from each family, our life is difficult. Our utility bills total 10 lingits a month, and our monthly rent on the longhouse is 120 lingits. We do not have money to live!

Having suddenly been plunged into a cash economy from a self-sufficient lifestyle, Chungdai is now struggling just to live.

Dr Hew Cheng Sim, a Malaysian sociologist, reported to the conference on Japanese ODA and Asian Women, held in 1995 in Tokyo, the results of her survey on the effects on Iban women of their forced displacement by the construction of the Batang Ai dam. She stated,

> Contrary to the legal custom of the Iban people, under which every family has land and property rights, compensation ranging from 10,000 to 40,000 lingits [from US$2,500 to $10,000], and a one-acre garden plot, were awarded to the heads of families, most of whom are men. The men, who had rarely seen such a large amount of cash, spent the money to purchase consumer items such as cars, motorbikes and electric appliances, or to take a *bejarai*, a trip of several months. Consequently, the women's economic power decreased sharply. Furthermore, because they had been robbed of the forest held as common property, the women lost the source of income they received from the forest by foraging for food, fuel and rattan used for weaving. Although women had always participated in the meetings of their longhouses equally alongside men, now only men are members of the development committee set up after their forced eviction. Thus, women have been driven into a subordinate position from the traditional gender equality they had enjoyed in Iban society.

The so-called modern development achieved with foreign capital which benefits the urban areas has destroyed the traditional Iban community solidarity and worsened women's situation. We have to ask "Whom does ODA benefit? Shouldn't it be for poor women?"

I went to see the Batang Ai Dam with women from the longhouse. Many treetops stuck up above the surface of the huge artificial lake, 8,500 hectares in size, built atop the 85-metre-high dam that serves as a hydroelectric power plant producing 108 megawatts of electric power. The women pointed to the other side of the lake, where their home town now lay under water, saying, "Our longhouse must be about there. We used to fish and bathe on the riverbank there."

Opposing Dam Construction

The government has made the decision to construct another huge dam in Sarawak. Indigenous people organized an opposition movement and, as a result, are suffering strong government suppression. The government intends to construct Bakun Dam on the upper tributary of the Rajang river. It will be the largest dam in Asia, producing

2,400 megawatts of electric power and covering 73,000 hectares, more than the total area of Singapore. Eighty per cent of the proposed site is untouched forest; fifteen villages of fifty-two longhouses, home to ten thousand indigenous people including the Kenya and the Kayan, will disappear to the bottom of the lake. When I visited one of those longhouses, Long Murung, located near Belaga, in 1987, Hanya, a Kayan woman, said anxiously,

> I never want to lose my field, the fruit trees that I have planted, my pigs and fish, and the precious forest. I have heard that the Iban people cannot live without money in the resettlement area. I talk with my husband, saying that I do not want to be like them.

Resistance against the construction of the Bakun dam was related to the groundswell of international resistance to the construction of huge dams. The massive Narmada Dam Project in India includes the construction of 30 large dams and 135 medium-sized dams that will cover 300,000 hectares of forest and 200,000 hectares of farmland. It will displace one million residents, a large number of them tribal minorities, who have campaigned against this project vociferously. Meda Patkar, 34, organized a nationwide network, The Association to Save Narmada, leading the resistance by conducting sit-ins and hunger strikes under the slogan "We won't permit destructive development!" despite repeated arrests. She requested that the Japanese government refuse to finance the project, and succeeded in obtaining the suspension of additional financing in 1990.

In China, the construction of the Three Gorges Dam on the Zhang river, which will be the third largest dam in the world, is progressing. A woman journalist, Tai Qing, voiced her protest in her book *The River Zhang! The River Zhang!*, written in 1989. She was arrested in the Tiananmen Square incident and, although released in 1990, was prohibited from publishing her book or criticizing the dam project. The construction of the dam was officially sanctioned in 1992. However, Tai Qing's appeal, "Protect the River Zhang, the Asian Treasure!" moved international opinion, and the World Bank and the US government decided to suspend financing of the project.

The role that women can play in raising questions and taking the lead in resisting the form of development symbolized by the construction of huge dams, which threatens the environment and the livelihood of the peoples of Asia, is vital.

Chapter 9

Taiwan and Thailand: The Other Side of the Travel Boom

Economic Development and Aborigines

The beautiful scenery of Taiwan, which is known as the Island of Beauty, attracts many tourists. Some Taiwanese people speak Japanese as a result of Japan's fifty years of colonial rule of Taiwan, which continued until 1945. This makes Japanese people feel close to Taiwan: over 800,000 Japanese tourists visited Taiwan in 1995. Well-known tourist spots in Taiwan include Wulai, Hualien, Wushe, Sun Moon Lake and Alishan, all of which are traditionally aboriginal areas. Initially, Taiwan aborigines were called *seiban* (savage tribesmen) by the Japanese colonial authority; after World War II, they were labelled Takasago tribes; then, under the Kuomintang (Chinese nationalist party) regime after the war, they were referred to as the Mountain People. Today, they call themselves Taiwan aborigines. The ten tribal groups, numbering over 300,000 people, make up less than 2 per cent of the total population of Taiwan. I wonder how aware tourists visiting Taiwan are of the hardships that these minorities have been forced to endure.

Taiwan has achieved rapid economic growth, calling global attention to itself as a leader of the NIEs. When I visited Taiwan at the end of the 1980s to attend the Conference on Asian Women, another Taiwan was revealed to me by Laya, a member of staff at the Aborigine Labour Centre, who guided me around Taipei, which was then experiencing a construction boom. Laya pointed out some of the construction sites, saying, "An aboriginal woman was killed in a construction accident here at the Sogo Department Store." "Eight aborigines died in construction accidents here during construction of the 36-floor Trade Centre Building, the tallest building in Taiwan." The wave of development reached the mountain areas, causing financial distress. Aboriginal people were forced to migrate to the urban areas to work as construction workers, where they occupied the bottom rung of the labour ladder and were sacrificed in labour accidents in the process. This is the severe reality aborigines have suffered.

With Laya, I visited an aboriginal people's area along a river in Shindian city, a suburb of Taipei. Laya told me, "Fifty-nine families came here from the mountain area and make their living as day workers. There is no electricity in this area, and they carry their water from the river." We could hear a woman's moans coming from one of the houses. The woman was suffering the aftereffects of giving birth without receiving proper medical care. Laya visited the young woman and uttered a fervent prayer for her. Later, she stated sadly, "Even though we appealed for compensation from the hospital for their medical slip-up, because they look down on aborigines, they did not take the appeal seriously."

Just as I was about to leave, I was very surprised to hear the mother-in-law of this young woman say, in very fluent Japanese, "Are you from Japan? Thank you very much for visiting my daughter-in-law." Since the aborigines received their education in Japanese during the Japanese colonial period, elderly people still use Japanese as a common language of communication among the various tribes.

An elderly man stuck his head out from the house next door, speaking to me in a friendly way in Japanese, saying, "My daughter is working in Tokyo." Laya told me, "She is probably working in a nightlife job. Young aboriginal women not only migrate to the cities in Taiwan to work; they also go to Japan to work."

Japanese Colonial Rule and Chinese Nationalism

The stories of the aborigines of Taiwan impressed me so much that I wrote a five-part series called "A Visit to the Tragic Mountain Areas: The Aborigines of Taiwan", which ran in the *Asahi Shimbun* from 21 to 29 October 1993. I wrote this series because I felt that I had to inform young Japanese people of Japan's oppression of the aborigines of Taiwan during the Japanese colonial period. This suppression is symbolized by the Wushe Uprising and also by Japan's organization during World War II of the Takasago Volunteer Corps, in which 6,000 aboriginal young men were sent to the frontline battlefield with the Japanese military forces, and over 3,000 lost their lives. For this, Japan must bear the responsibility.

Dr Warisutem, a member of the Atayal aboriginal group, whom I met at a clinic in Wushe, told me, "The land which was the reservation set aside for the aborigines was handed over to the ethnic Chinese majority and used for tourist resorts, tea plantations, horse-radish plantations and industrial sites. Development has proceeded on the land taken from us, but we can no longer survive in the mountain areas." Dr Warisutem is one of the leaders of the abor-igines' rights movement, which grew out of the rise of ethnic consciousness in the 1970s.

In the Wushe Uprising in 1930, the Atayal aboriginal people revolted, dissatisfied with Japan's control of the aborigines in Taiwan. They attacked the Japanese on a sports day at a Japanese elementary school and killed 134 Japanese people. Japan dispatched its military forces and, using modern military weapons, cruelly slaughtered the Atayal people. I visited a woman who survived the Wushe Incident – her Chinese name is Gao Zaiyun, her Atayal name Obintadao, and her Japanese name Takayama Hatsuko – at the Lushan Hot Springs, located above Wushe. Now over 80 years old, she remains a beautiful woman with a dignified bearing. In very polite Japanese, she told me her painful life story, of the group suicide of twenty-four family members, including her 20-year-old husband. Pregnant, Obintadao was told to survive in order to pass on the history to succeeding generations.

With the son whom she was expecting at the time of the group suicide, Obintadao runs a small inn. Although there used to be only two or three inns at Lushan Hot Springs, there now stand over thirty luxury hotels, most of which are owned by the ethnic Chinese. She expressed her concern, saying, "The aboriginal people's land is gradually being taken away. I wonder how much longer we can continue to operate our inn." The land where the Atayal sacrificed their lives resisting Japan, where her family's blood was shed and where she has lived with painful memories for more than eighty years, this holy land will also be taken as a result of the ethnic Chinese tourism development boom. Over half of the aborigines

Gao Zaiyun (Obintadao) with her son, recounting her painful life story

have left their native mountain areas, no longer able to make a living there, and moved to the plains. The men have become construction workers, coalminers or crew members on deep-sea fishing boats, where they experience discrimination, exploitation and poverty.

I visited the village of Tappan in Alishan, a tourist spot well known to the Japanese, inhabited by the Tsou aboriginal group. It was from this village that an 18-year-old boy was deceived and hired by a Taipei laundry shop. Unable to bear the cruel treatment and humiliation he suffered, he finally murdered all three members of the shop-owner's family Although a movement arose to save his life, conducted by those who believed that this tragedy happened because of ethnic discrimination, the death penalty was quickly carried out. When I learned about the case, I wanted to visit the parents of the boy.

His village commanded a breathtaking view of the mountains, and a Tsou song could be heard, a song so beautiful that the village singers were invited to Paris to perform it. The overall effect was that of a veritable paradise. But in total contrast to the peaceful scenery was the indescribable pain endured by the parents of the boy. I was at a loss for words, especially when I learned about the mother's life. A woman doctor, she had suffered a traffic accident just before her son had murdered his employer's family. Her injured legs keep her from travelling around the village to visit her patients. In addition, since her father was a Tsou leader, he was thought to have collaborated with the Japanese and so was assassinated by the Kuomintang after the war. This woman, who had experienced the tragic deaths of both her father and her son, said, "I have to over- come my sadness and live strongly!" Then she smiled as she left for her clinic; assisted in getting on her motorbike, she rode away.

Leaving the village, my car passed a truck filled with people. An elderly man, speaking to me in Japanese, explained, "We are going out to harvest horseradish, which is exported to Japan." I was told that he is the uncle of the executed boy and a former soldier in the Japanese military. I heard that many young people from this village were called up by the Japanese and died in battle. The horseradish plantations, covering the mountains up to the very top, are owned by the ethnic Chinese, who hire the Tsou tribal people as agri- cultural workers, paying them very low wages. I brooded over the strange reality of the tragic secret of the village of the Tsou and its current connection with Japan through the production and export of horseradish.

Using Women as Tourist Traps

Wulai, twenty-seven kilometres southeast of Taipei, a tourist spot known for its white-water falls and hot springs, welcomes 400,000 to 500,000 tourists every year. The exotic, beautiful, fair-skinned young girls of an Atayual village nearby are used by the tourist industry as an added attraction. There was a time when most of the young women in the village became prostitutes, and many women have children fathered by foreign men, including the Japanese. The middle-aged woman of whom I happened to ask the way told me in fluent Japanese, "My two daughters married Japanese men and live in Japan."

Dropping in at the Atayal Aborigines' Culture Theatre, a stop on the Wulai tourism route, I saw that the hall was filled with Japanese and Korean tourists. Young Atayal girls, dressed in gorgeous traditional costumes, filled the stage, dancing and singing. Although young women entertainers are not involved in prostitution, as was once the case, they are still used as a resource which brings income from tourists to the village.

Mo Na neng, a visually handicapped poet of the Paiwan tribe and spiritual leader of the aboriginal movement, complained to me, "In order to attract tourists, the dancers' skirts have been shortened to make them appear sexy, and the music has been arranged discotheque-style. It has become a show rather than an introduction to the traditional culture of the aborigines." In a well-known poem, "When the Bell Rings", which was dedicated to the girls in mountain areas who are forced into prostitution, he bemoaned the sacrifice of the aboriginal girls to trafficking. He himself is from a poor village in the south, having worked in the depths of poverty and lost his eyesight after experiencing every hardship in life. His younger sister was sold to a brothel; thus, his poem communicates deep grief in every single line. He read the poem at the meeting of the International Year of Indigenous People in Taipei in May 1993, and in his clear, resonant voice, the sobs of the mountain tribal people throughout the nation could be heard.

In Hualien, a tourist spot on the eastern seashore, the Good Shepherd Centre receives young girls who are the victims of trafficking. At the centre were eight Taroko girls, ranging in age from 11 to 17 years old. I was told that they were sold in Shuilin District, the Taroko area that stretches along the mountainous side of Hualien. Three of the eight are sisters, and the oldest, at 17, is working hard to become a hairdresser. A social worker said,

> She was sold to a brothel in Taipei when she was 11 years old; there she was confined for three years. She was taken into police custody and stayed in a protection centre for two years. She returned to her village only to be sold again to a brothel in Taipei. She was brought here by the police six months later. No matter how often we rescue these girls and help them return home, they will only be sold again, depending on the home situation, such as poverty or the father's alcoholism; thus, nothing is changed.

I was told that this girl has studied at beauty school so seriously that she is now able to live at the beauty salon and work.

I also heard about a 16-year-old girl who, after she was orphaned, was repeatedly sold by an aunt. In another case, two girls were sold

by their father after their mother left home. A member of staff at
the centre said,

> Since the government has placed priority on economic development at
> the expense of the lives of the aborigines, many of them are driven
> to poverty and lose hope in the future; the men drown themselves in
> drink and sell their daughters to get money to buy alcohol. According
> to a police report, 116 girls below the age of 16 have disappeared in
> the past four months. Girls are sold to brothels not only here in
> Hualien, but also to brothels in Taipei.

I walked around Huaxi Street, close to the Longshan Temple, located
southwest of Taipei Station. Brothels line the narrow alleys running
from north to south and east to west. There, the women working
in prostitution were attempting to entice clients. They were girls
dressed in simple clothing and wearing heavy make-up. Many of
them were easily recognizable as aboriginal girls by their features.

Lin Mei-Jung, who is involved in the aborigine support movement, reports,

> At least 20 per cent, and in some areas up to 40 per cent, of the
> women working in prostitution in Taipei are aborigines. Considering
> that these groups compose only less than 2 per cent of the total
> population of Taiwan, this is an extraordinarily high ratio.

In the 1980s, a Taiwan women's group issued an appeal to the public
by carrying out demonstrations in this area, demanding, "Don't sell
and don't buy girls from the mountain areas." Then, the same group
founded the Rainbow Project to support them. However, it is not
easy to protect aborigine girls from the prostitution industry, which
is flourishing due to Taiwan's economic growth, as they hold the
weakest position in society.

In the Shadow of Resort Development

Thailand, The Land of Smiles, visited by 6 million tourists from
throughout the world each year, is the kingdom of tourism in Asia.
The Thai government, which launched its tourism-promotion policy
to gain foreign exchange in the 1970s, initiated the successful "Visit
Thailand Year" in 1987 and has continued to promote tourism
nationwide ever since.

In the north, the ancient city of Chiang Mai became an international tourist centre with the advent of international flights. Then the tourism boom spread northward. In 1992, an international airport was constructed at Chiang Rai, with direct flights from Narita Airport in Japan. Chiang Rai International Airport has become the gateway to the Golden Triangle, which has developed into a new tourism mecca in northern Thailand.

Along the Golden Triangle calmly flows the Mekong river. On one side lies Laos, and on the other side is Burma. The borders of the three countries of Thailand, Laos and Burma all meet here. Formerly an area cultivating plants to produce drugs, it has been transformed into an international resort area featuring luxury hotels and golf courses.

The Japanese government cooperated with this tourism development through ODA financing, contributing 1.1 billion yen (US$8 million) in loans for road construction from Maesai, on the Burmese border, through the Golden Triangle to Cheng Seng, an ancient city, and 30 million yen for the restoration of the ruins of Cheng Seng and other projects.

However, the sites of the tourist highways are the traditional areas of the hill-tribe minority groups. I will never forget the shock I experienced when I visited these villages. In many houses, couples lay smoking opium from early morning until late at night. The children sitting beside them lacked the energy even to utter a cry, they were so hungry. There were no schools, no clinics and no young women. This posed for me a fundamental question about using ODA for the development of tourism. I wondered whether we shouldn't have prioritized alleviating the poverty of the people in this area rather than providing good facilities for tourists from rich countries.

Pipat Chaisurin, a former teacher of elementary school in hill-tribe villages for eighteen years who became a tour guide, criticized this kind of tourism development, saying, "The hill-tribe people are being used as a tourism resource. Young girls are sold for the tourists and trekking tourists involve the hill-tribe people in drugs. I cannot allow the hill-tribe people to be sacrificed for tourism any longer." Pipat established Maekock Farm on the side of a river one hour's boat ride northeast of Chiang Rai to help hill-tribe people recover from drug abuse and regain self-sufficiency. His wife, Anuluk, is making efforts to set up a textile project to provide income for the hill-tribe women. Japanese citizens support the project of this couple, who received training at Asia Rural Institute in Japan.

Phuket Island, located in the south of Thailand facing the Indian Ocean, is an internationally popular resort known as Paradise Island. However, for the people of Phuket Island, all of this is very troubling, especially for the Chaore minority people, who have been driven into hardship by tourism. Even though they have lived on their land for a long time, they do not have title to it, and so they are about to be driven off it by tourist development, as are other indigenous people in Asia. Visiting one of the four Chaore villages, I heard a 90-year-old woman say in desperation, "I want to die on this land where we have lived for such a long time."

Nui, a woman in her twenties, who accompanied me, is a leader of the Phuket Environment Protection Club and a campaign to protect the island; she was wearing a T-shirt which states, "Yesterday's Paradise, Tomorrow's Hell." She said,

> Most of the seacoasts of the island have been developed as resort beaches, and we, the residents of the island, have been prohibited from entering the beaches. At the very least, we want to protect the northwest seashore, which is still undeveloped, from the development plans of foreign capital.

Nui organized a ten-day sit-in at a temple, held a hunger strike and even organized a 3,000-person demonstration. She declared,

> Our island has been taken away from us by foreign tourists. The environmental pollution is worsening. Why do we, the residents of this island, have to suffer so? Although my mother tells me to stop my activity because it is dangerous, I cannot stop the struggle to protect our island!"

Nui's strong determination moved students in Bangkok, who appealed directly to the prime minister. Consequently, the development in the northern part of Phuket Island was suspended pending reconsideration. I fear that people who enjoy their vacations on Phuket Island are totally unaware of the anger and the actions of this young woman.

Golf Courses for Farms

You can see the Japanese in tourist areas throughout the world, whether the place is famous or not. In 1995, the number of Japanese taking trips abroad exceeded 15 million. From 1985, when the number of Japanese travelling abroad reached 5 million, the number tripled in a brief ten-year period. The destination of 75 per cent of Japanese overseas tourists is Asia and the Pacific region, with the number-one destination being Hawaii, a part of the USA, but located in the Pacific geographically. The second choice is Korea, Japan's neighbour, followed by Taiwan and Hong Kong. In addition, the number of tourists from the NIE countries has increased dramatically, and sex tours are no longer exclusive to Japanese men.

The popularization of consumer culture in the form of sight-seeing tours abroad is promoting the policy of international tourist development in the receiving countries. The local governments and businesses always emphasize the three merits of increasing tourism: the acquisition of foreign currency; the creation of employment opportunities; and the expansion of regional development. The governments of the North, the World Bank and TNCs are strengthening their control over tourism.

The Japanese government estimates that the number of Japanese travellers abroad will reach 20 million by the end of the twentieth century, and it is promoting a policy of ODA for tourism as a part of its international cooperation. JICA is even engaged in developing a tourist development master plan for Thailand and Malaysia, and it supports tourism facilities through yen loans of ODA in many areas, including northern Thailand. Japanese business enterprises are also becoming involved in the development of tourist resort facilities, including airports, hotels and golf courses in various parts of Asia.

However, the serious consequences that such tourism development has for local people, already described in this chapter, include the exploitation of land and natural resources, pollution of the environment, expansion of prostitution, inflation and the commercialization of culture, which constitute direct attacks on indigenous people, women, children, farmers and fisherfolk.

One example of this is the construction of golf courses, which the peoples of the Asia-Pacific Region in such places as Indonesia, the Philippines, Hawaii and Guam strongly oppose, saying, "Don't take our farms away from us!" "Don't waste our precious resources of water and electricity!" and "Don't destroy our historic ruins!" Japan has already constructed more than two thousand golf courses domestically and it cannot build any more at home. Now it has started to export golf courses just as it formerly exported pollution. In 1993, an Asian Anti-Golf-Course Conference was held in Penang, Malaysia, and a Global Network on Golf Course Issues was formed.

The movement has grown to monitor the global issues resulting from the expanding international tourist industry, which has become the second largest global industry after that of petroleum. In the 1980s, the Ecumenical Coalition on Third World Tourism was organized in Bangkok. It acts in cooperation with networks in Europe and the USA. The Third World Tourism Forum, held on Phuket Island in 1992, resolved to fight the violence against human dignity caused by tourism.

The Conference on the Effects of Tourism on Indigenous Hawaiians, held in Hawaii in 1989, was followed by the Asian Conference on Tourism and Aborigines, held in Taiwan. It issued a statement that declared,

> The aborigines themselves should control tourism in order to uphold their rights, their dignity, and their survival. We resist any tourism development that does not have the approval and participation of local people.

What serious problems are created for the receiving countries and people when we enjoy overseas travel? Are we not too insensitive to this issue? Tourist development involves critical North–South issues.

Part III

From Resistance
to Alternatives in Action

Banana-packing centre in Negros

Chapter 10

An Alternative Negros: The Philippines

Famine Island

The Negros Campaign celebrated its tenth anniversary in 1996. This sugar-cane-producing island of the Philippines has become closely related to Japan as a result of the its banana trade. The former image of starving children is fading and is being replaced by one of smiling children. This has been achieved by cooperation between the people of Negros and the people of Japan in creating the Negros Alternative. I realized the significance of the women's role in Negros when I made my third trip to this island, with the Women's Study Tour (see Chapter 2) in April 1996.

In 1985, UNICEF reported, "The lives of 1.4 million children are at risk", and called for international aid for Negros Island, which was in a state of famine due to the sudden fall in the international price of sugar. More than a quarter of the 260,000 sugar plantation workers lost their jobs, and hundreds of thousands of people, including workers' family members, were deprived of their livelihood. Starvation attacked children especially, as those in the most vulnerable position.

When this tragic news became known in Japan, Japanese people who had been involved in Filipino issues organized the Japanese Committee for Negros Campaign (JCNC) on 25 February 1986, the very day that then-President Marcos fled abroad and his long dictatorship was toppled by Filipino citizens. JCNC aimed at alternative aid based not on one-way charity, as in the case of aid for starving Africa, but on support for achievement of equal partnership. The first step towards this goal was to call for nationwide emergency financial contributions to supply food. JCNC conducted support activities in cooperation with people's organizations in Negros. It not only campaigned for emergency contributions but also cooperated with activities to enable Negros citizens to become self-sufficient.

I visited Negros for the first time in the spring of 1988, two years after the foundation of JCNC. I will never forget the scene in the hospital I visited in Bacolod city, the capital of Negros Occidental. The children and babies I saw lying on beds in the paediatric ward were so thin, it looked as if they could break in two. Their large, vacant, sunken eyes peered out from pale faces. They lay exhausted, lacking the energy even to cry. I recall the downhearted faces of the mothers as they looked upon their children. One mother held up her son as she spoke through her tears: "I did not have any food to give him. I want him to receive medical treatment and be saved by all means!" The child was 2 years old, and although the average weight for a child this age is 12 kilogrammes, he only weighed 4.5. The number of children who died of malnutrition in this hospital was 210 in 1986, 188 in 1987 and over 200 in 1988. This means that every three days, two children died in this hospital alone; we have no way of calculating how many children died of malnutrition throughout Negros Island, including those who died in other medical institutions and those who died without receiving any medical care.

In response to my question about how such starvation could happen on this abundantly verdant island, Melanie, a woman staff member of the Negros Rescue and Restoration Centre, who was my guide, responded by giving me some historical background. "This was a human-made famine. The people of Negros have been forced to grow nothing but sugar cane ever since the Spanish colonial period." All of the land in Negros has been in the hands of the large-scale plantation landowners, and the vast majority of people have not even owned land on which to produce their own food.

Sugar-cane plantations were introduced in Negros in the 1850s, and Negros has produced 70 per cent of the sugar exported by the Philippines; this has led to Negros being called the Sugar Bowl of the Philippines. Some 3 million people live on this island, of whom 70 per cent are dependent on sugar-cane production. In fact the plantation workers and their families have been treated like slaves for the past 150 years. Only about 2 per cent of the population of Negros owns almost all the private land of the island, and 80 per cent of the population live below the poverty line. This typical system of large landownership, and the resulting gap between rich and poor, epitomizes Philippine society.

In this situation, in which sugar-cane workers were barely surviving, plantation owners drastically reduced the acreage of sugar-cane production in response to the sudden drop in the price of sugar on the world market. Workers lost their jobs and their families were soon driven to starvation. This was not a natural disaster; it was a human-made disaster. However, the people of Negros refused to give in to the hardship fate had dealt them; rather, they rose to their feet to launch a struggle for their very survival.

The Banana Project

Taking a jeepney and heading north from Bacolod city, I passed a vast area of shrimp cultivation that stretched along the coast. Beginning in 1986, a shrimp cultivation boom occurred when sugar-cane plantation owners began to switch over from the production of sugar cane, following the sharp drop in the price of sugar. In 1991, the amount of land given over to shrimp cultivation in Negros reached 6,000 hectares with Negros producing 70 per cent of all cultivated shrimp in the Philippines. Melanie stated angrily,

> Seventy per cent of the shrimp produced here are exported to Japan, despite the reality of the food shortage and the starving children in Negros. Once plantation land is changed into shrimp cultivation ponds, the land can never again be used as agricultural land, due to the use of sea water mixed with underground water in the shrimp cultivation ponds. Because shrimp cultivation does not require intensive labour, it is not a solution to unemployment either.

I visited a sugar-cane plantation located beyond Silay town, forty kilometres north of Bacolod city. A mother of two children pointed out of the window of her nipa palm hut, saying, "Last year a hundred mothers each put out 13 pesos [US20¢] to establish a co-op store, stocking rice, salt and oil. Although the co-op's income gradually increased and all of us were so happy with it, the military threatened us and we had to close the co-op store six months later."

Neighbourhood women came together for a meeting, bringing their children. "It was a great experience for us women working together to improve and make our lives just a little happier. When peace returns to our island, we will open our co-op store again." Declaring that their efforts have been only temporarily suspended, these women, who have gained a sense of self-sufficiency and confidence for the first time, have no intention of giving up.

JCNC supports over fifty such projects, all mini-projects to achieve self-sufficiency for workers, poor farmers, fisherfolk and squatters, through cooperative cultivation of rice, vegetables and fruit, collective raising of livestock and joint operation of a basic co-op store. Women play a large role in many of these projects; however, some projects failed due to the Aquino administration's "total war policy" against guerrilla forces. In spite of such a severe situation, some women who lost their jobs opened food shops or started sewing projects.

The beginning of the 1990s witnessed the birth of a totally new and unique action programme to achieve self-sufficiency, the Banana Project. The purpose of my second visit to Negros, in 1992, was to witness this new project first-hand. My destination was a village cultivating bananas in the mountainous region of Mount Canraon, located in the central part of Negros Island. From Lagranha town, at the foot of the mountain, the car climbed up a gravel road through the sugar-cane plantations; then we walked up the steep mountain road for another hour. Along the way, I passed villagers, their bodies covered with sweat, carrying sixty to seventy kilogrammes of green bananas in baskets suspended from yokes across their shoulders. Everyone from young women to children breathed heavily as they came down the steep slope carrying the bananas. I realized anew how much hard labour goes into producing every single banana.

I finally reached the Vaice district, where Eva Batelna, 44, chairperson of the Balangon Growers' Association (BGA), founded the previous year, welcomed me with a smile. Although a mother of five children, she was actively involved in the activities of the first agricultural cooperative in Negros. Balangon is actually the name of the variety of banana that is grown on the slopes of the Negros mountains. It is a full-flavoured banana that has been grown naturally without the use of fertilizers or agricultural chemicals, and exported to Japan through the people-to-people banana trade since

1990. The BGA is the producers' organization, which now has a hundred member families.

"Since we began to grow Balangon bananas cooperatively for export to Japan, our lives have become much easier." According to Eva, the monthly income, previously 500 to 600 pesos, has tripled. Consequently, BGA members can now have three meals a day, send their children to school, repair their houses, and they are liberated from having to work as plantation workers. "What pleases me most is seeing the growing sense of community and caring for one another in our village", exclaimed Eva, speaking with the pride of a leader.

One Japanese Woman's Surprise

Kayano Harada, a member of the Association of Women to Create the Future of Okitama, located in Yamagata Prefecture, who visited this banana-cultivation area, wrote in her report,

> In Negros, women are leaders. Although our rural area of Japan has various producers' co-op associations, the chairpersons and executive members are 100 per cent male. We join the co-ops as family units, but the representative of each family is always a man. Coming from such a world, I was surprised to see the banana producers' organization in Negros. I wondered why, and asked Banji, 42, the first BGA chairperson. I learned that in the Philippines, women are allowed to speak out equally in the democratic setting of the home, so women can also be active without experiencing discrimination in their local communities.

The first three chairpersons of the BGA have all been women. "Because men have to work outside the home, it is the women who are engaged in community affairs", said Eva. She guided me to a nearby site where bananas were being harvested. It was the men who, with large mountain knives, skilfully cut dark green bunches of heavy bananas and piled them into large baskets. As I had seen before, both men and women were carrying bananas half-way down the mountain to the collecting point.

From there, the bananas are transported to the packing centre in Lagranha town by car, washed one by one, dried, labelled and boxed by hand by workers who include residents of the nearby slums and the unemployed workers. Many of them are women, from young

Eva on the way to the harvest area, with male workers

girls to middle-aged women. Marelina, 46, who works in quality control at the packing centre, said,

> I was exploited as a child worker from the time I was 10 years old. I married and bore nine children, but I was unable to feed them adequately or provide the needed medical care, so I lost four. Because I was not able to endure the severe conditions on the plantation, I became involved in trade union activities, and as a result, I was fired three years ago. Since there are so many unemployed people, we decided that we would share the job opportunities here, so the centre has a work-sharing system by which people from four hundred families work in turn.

Because of this work-sharing system, a non-competitive and non-market economic structure is maintained here.

The bananas, packed in boxes, are transported by air from Bacolod to Manila, and then sent to Japan by ship. They are sent to over twenty Negros campaign networks, consumer co-ops and other consumer groups throughout Japan. This system results in a 20 yen

(US$15) profit on every kilo of bananas sold, which goes into a fund to achieve self-sufficiency in Negros. Alter Trade, the people's trading company, which began by shipping a mere 80 tonnes of bananas to Japan in 1989, shipped a total of 1,500 tonnes in 1993.

However, although the banana trade expanded, it encountered several difficulties, including both damage from several typhoons that hit Negros and the spread of a viral plant disease in 1993. The virus spread as a result of successive plantings without giving the soil a rest. In order to fulfil the demand for bananas in Japan, many people started to compete in cultivating bananas, and consequently, the number of banana palms in Negros jumped from 300,000 to 600,000 within only a few years. This placed a heavy burden on the Negros soil, which had already been depleted due to a hundred and fifty years of concentrated single-crop sugar-cane production, which served to destroy the ecosystem. However, the BGA producers were undaunted by this crisis; rather, they turned this hardship into an opportunity to move forward:

> We have become too dependent on bananas as a means of achieving self-sufficiency. We've decided to engage in organic farming and live in harmony with the environment. We need to begin to engage in subsistence farming that makes use of a cyclic system of rice and vegetable production, livestock breeding and compost production to enrich the soil.

The alternative agriculture plan was launched in 1994, led by 39-year-old Chita Takata, who became the third BGA chairperson. After her husband was murdered by the military, Chita raised her three children alone and became active in BGA:

> Although we have depended on support from outsiders and NGOs, we are now trying to become truly self-sufficient farmers. Even if the BGA is an agricultural organization, we are not real farmers as long as we have to buy our rice. We do not want to always be beneficiaries of NGOs; but we want to be self-directed and want to achieve by ourselves.

Encouraging others with her inherent enthusiasm, Chita has led the BGA in branching out to plant rice and corn.

The People's Plan for the 21st Century (PP-21) is a new movement, organized in 1996, to spread this spirit throughout the Philippines, beginning in Negros, in order to build a new democratic people's movement. It aims at achieving the self-sufficiency of the Negros people by an alternative form of development that is based on people-power agriculture and fishing, and resists development and industrialization promoted by the government and TNCs. PP-21 has already begun in seven locations, including sugar-cane plantation land recovered from landlords, mountain villages, banana-cultivation areas, fishing villages and urban slums. Women form the leadership of this movement. I encountered the breath of fresh air that is this movement when I participated in the Women's Study Tour in April 1996.

Exchange Programmes with Other Women's Organizations

Women's Initiatives for Social Empowerment (WISE), which received our Women's Study Tour in Negros, is a women's NGO in Negros founded in 1994 to promote women's empowerment.

> To achieve self-sufficiency in Negros, a gender – in other words, women's – viewpoint and a concern for the environment are essential. In order to speak out and act on issues that women at the grassroots feel are of concern in daily life, we provide workshops in local areas. We have five staff who work to raise consciousness and organize women

declared Dionera Madrona, 38, the chairperson of WISE, who has acted on behalf of peasants' and women's movements for many years. She is the mother of three children; her first husband was murdered, and her second husband is the manager of the factory processing muscovado sugar which is exported to Japan and other countries in people's trade.

Dionera took me to the Napoles Farm, located about one hour by car south of Bacolod; there, the women's group BANAWA was formed with WISE support. Villagers began planting rice on the 78 hectares of sugar-cane land they finally acquired as a result of their struggle for ownership. The village was so poor that there was not a stick of furniture in the nipa palm farmhouses; still, its women were vibrantly alive.

"We raise pigs and ducks to produce income", they said, as they gave me some duck eggs. BANAWA members run a credit union to which each member contributes 50 centavos a day. They also discuss issues related to children's education. Every day is an exciting new experience, especially for women in poverty who have never before expressed an opinion in front of other people.

Linda, the chairperson of the committee, is a calm, gentle woman over 60 years of age. She said, "Although I was very lonely after my husband died, since we organized our women's group and we always help each other, I am very happy." The twenty-one members of our Women's Study Tour split into several small groups to spend the night at several farmhouses. We were all impressed with the strong will of the village women, who, in the midst of poverty, are always trying to look toward the future with hope. Dionera, the WISE chairperson, said, "To empower women at grassroots level all over Negros, to rebuild our island by our own strength: this is the role WISE is called on to play."

Since the Negros campaign began, one Filipino woman, Dessa Quesada, 30, has visited Japan many times to appeal for support for the campaign, performing music and drama nationwide. Since 1994, Dessa, who has worked in the international department of Rural and Urban Alternative Plan (RUAP), an NGO in Tokyo, says,

> Women in Negros suffer from famine and natural disasters, and are victims of economic exploitation and military oppression. After their men were killed, the women were strengthened by their struggle, which enabled them and their children to survive. Now, the islanders are making every effort through PAP to change the sugar-cane island into an island of subsistence agriculture, the leaders in this effort being women. We cannot build a future without women's power!

Dessa coordinated a workshop, Asian Women's Alternatives in Action, at the Beijing conference NGO Forum, in order to share the wonderful experiences of the women of Negros with the world. She is now engaged in an effort to establish an Asian Women's Alternatives in Action Committee, a women's network to create a new future for Asia with the cooperation of Japanese women's groups.

Negros has been in transition from an island of famine, mourning and tears to an island of hope and self-reliance for more than ten years. The women of Negros who have supported this transition provide great encouragement for other Asian women.

Chapter 11

Women's Linkage:
Hong Kong and China

A Poor Mountain Village in Jiangxi Province

"You can see that the village women are actively engaged in washing lily bulbs, can't you? Although men used to dominate everything in this village, now women have founded a credit union all by themselves and are working to build village prosperity." At the workshop on Asian Women's Alternatives in Action at the Beijing women's conference NGO Forum, Lau Kin Chi, 40, passed around a bag of lily-bulb powder, showed a video and reported on the women's self-reliance project in a mountain village in Jiangxi Province in China. Her presentation attracted participants' interest.

Lau teaches comparative literature at Linnan University in Hong Kong and also acts as a leader in ARENA, an NGO that considers alternative development for Asia. In addition, with friends who are involved with China issues, she founded another NGO in 1993, the China Social Service Development Research Centre (CSD), to begin supporting grassroots people's development in mainland China. She is an activist, her tiny body overflowing with energy; she is also a theorist with a broad viewpoint and perceptive insight.

Wanting to hear more about her activities, we invited Lau to the symposium Create Women's Alternatives, held in Enoshima in May 1996, sponsored by the Asia–Japan Women's Resource Centre. She reported in detail on her project in China:

> China's economy is developing rapidly since the change to a market economy under the open reform policy in 1978. Meanwhile, the gap between rich and poor has widened, and especially agricultural

villages have become impoverished. Therefore CSD chose to support women's programmes to achieve self-reliance in the poverty-stricken, remote areas.

After holding discussions with the Women's Federation in Jiangxi Province, pilot projects started in the two villages of Luxia and Wanli in 1994. Lau described the conditions she found when she visited the two villages for the first time:

> The villages are located seven hours by bus from Nanchang, the provincial capital. Then you have to walk the rough mountain road, which is often closed because of landslides. It is a remote mountain area, and the only way the ten thousand people living there can make contact with the outside world is by the area's one phone. Living in the most impoverished area, villagers' average annual income is only 520 yuan [US$65]. Their lifelong suffering is completely untouched by economic development.

Realizing that nothing could happen without capital, Lau and her colleagues suggested that the first step should be the establishment of a women's credit union. As one of the means to enable women in developing countries to achieve self-reliance, the establishment of credit unions is seen as vital. They visited all 290 homes in the two villages and explained the proposal in detail. Although 80 per cent of the village men knew about the presence of a government-approved credit union there, none of the women knew about the credit union as it is administered by the heads of families, men.

> Some women felt that the credit unions were men's responsibility. Village customs dictated that it is only men who participate in public affairs, including village meetings, and make all the decisions. This resulted in an atmosphere in which it was difficult for women to speak out, due to their suppression by the male village mayor and the local party leaders.

The same patriarchal structure exists in Japanese agricultural villages.

The Women's Co-op Credit Union

Lau told the village women about women's activities in other Asian countries, convincing them that "we women can also achieve"; in the process, they gained confidence. The village women showed even greater interest in a women's credit union than anticipated,

and fifty women came to the first meeting to discuss its formation.
They established the policy that all decisions would be made jointly.
Lau reported,

> The women discussed at great length whether the membership of the
> credit union should be held by the family or the individual. Someone
> raised the question as to why women are always referred to as
> someone's wife, daughter, daughter-in-law or mother, and the result
> of the discussion was the decision that the members would be the
> individual women. Following this rule, families with more women
> members will benefit. Someone even joked that although women's
> existence has never been welcomed in rural society, they will be
> welcomed hereafter.

A wide variety of opinions was also expressed during the discussion regarding how to choose the credit union leaders. They determined that they would select the executive members by vote, after
establishing the qualifications for office: a leader would have to be
an honest person who would never use credit union funds for
personal gain, a person who has received enough education to make
out a balance sheet, a person who has enough time to give to the
union and a person who does not have her own agenda, but who
makes public what is going on. Some women in the villages who
had never voted before experienced true democracy in action. Thus,
the women's co-op credit union was established by seventy-five
members who contributed one yuan (US10¢) each.

The women decided to raise funds by cultivating lily bulbs, taking
a tip from the people's banana trade between Negros and Japan.
Jiangxi Province has been well known for the production of lily
bulbs. Villagers traditionally mix dried lily-bulb powder with water
or hot water to drink as a health food. The lily bulbs cultivated by
the villagers used to be purchased by influential members of society
to be processed in their factories. The credit union started to buy
these lily bulbs, wash, pack and grind them into powder as a cooperative venture. Then the credit union started to sell the products
directly to consumers in Hong Kong in what has become grassroots
or alternative trade.

> Making use of the summer vacation, the women credit union
> members work together at the village elementary school. When asked
> why the village men did not come to help, some women answered

that the men were at home baby-sitting and cooking. This change symbolizes a landmark in the history of this village.

Thus, in the summer of 1994, a truck containing four tonnes of fresh vacuum-packed lily bulbs arrived in Hong Kong. "It was not easy to sell them in the shopping areas. But about a hundred students and other volunteers did their best and succeeded in selling all the lily bulbs." This became an incentive for young people who were interested in this project to visit the village and set up an exchange between Hong Kong and the villages. Green Empowerment was founded as a sister organization of CSD. This new group accepted the responsibility for lily bulb trade and sales. It not only took as its task enlarging Green Empowerment's consumer network in Hong Kong, but also set out to establish an Asian network of consumers and producers.

The Lily Bulb Trade

The first shipment of lily bulbs netted 40,000 yuan (US$5,000) in profit. The credit union members discussed how to divide the profits. Finally, they decided to pay 160 yuan ($20) to each member and use the rest for a credit union activity fund and an education fund. The profit distributed to each person is equal to one-third of the average annual income, so it represents quite a significant amount. From the second year, the credit union deposited 50 per cent of the profit in the credit union activity fund, divided 30 per cent among the individual members and invested 20 per cent in the education fund.

The women credit union members started to improve village life by making use of credit union funds. They revitalized what had been virtually a dormant village. Pooling their strength, the women opened a daycare centre on village land, established classes in literacy and agricultural skills, purchased flour-milling and threshing machines, rented farmland to produce fruits and vegetables, piped spring water to the village through bamboo pipes, subscribed to a women's newspaper and established a fund to support families in poverty. Women have achieved all these things within only two years. The smiling women's faces seen in the video are brimming with confidence.

This has truly achieved the goal of empowering women. Women had been told that they were incompetent and incapable of doing anything, and they themselves believed it was true. But seeing the profit they had made in raising lily bulbs and all that they had achieved, they gained confidence. Due to their success, the number of credit union members increased to ninety-four, with most of the village women of working age becoming members of the credit union.

Although the women who had remained silent under the authority of male village executives and the village chapter of the Women's Federation have now became empowered enough to change the entire village, they have encountered many difficulties:

> The first was the problem related to having been accustomed to a vertical social hierarchy for a long period of time. Many women were not even able to make decisions for themselves and they were accustomed to waiting always to receive directions from their superiors. We had to exert efforts to avoid establishing a precedent of the chairperson making all the decisions and instead establish the custom of everyone participating in the democratic decision-making process.

The second problem to address was that of mutual distrust:

> They have experienced an unending series of governmental campaigns including the Great Leap Forward, collectivization and the Great Cultural Revolution, after which they have been exposed to a completely different social value system including individualism and competition during the last ten or more years. Due to this series of drastic changes, interpersonal relationships have been destroyed. Now we have to overcome the mutual distrust among villagers, which is a very difficult thing to do.

The third problem was a tendency to seek short-term profits:

> They are concerned about the possibility of changes in government policy. They have developed a philosophy of getting whatever they can while they have the chance. Thus, four or five credit union members suggested that purchasing a charcoal-producing machine would be more profitable than buying a flour mill with credit union funds. One third of the members agreed with this proposal, but finally the opinion that buying a flour mill would be more useful for all members received the majority vote.

Eliminating Domestic Violence

Farmers who have had to endure poverty resulting from forced collectivism imposed from above welcomed the liberalization that resulted from the reform policy. However, as a result of the severe

competition that ensued, farmers have had to work harder and harder
to survive, and those on whom the greatest burden has been placed
have been women. Therefore the women promoted voluntary
democratic collectivism, the credit union, proposed by Lau and her
colleagues.

> Women in the two villages of Luxia and Wanli came together to act.
> Those who used to work separately even in the same village came
> together to help one another. This is collectivism in the best sense.
> The change in the relationship between men and women is an even
> greater fruit of this movement

emphasized Lau strongly.

> Legally, men and women are equal in China. However, in actuality,
> women's status at home is low. For example, husbands' violence used
> to exist in credit union members' homes. However, since the women
> founded the credit union, the issue of gender equality has been given
> serious consideration, and the problem of patriarchy has been
> addressed. Women who suffer their husband's violence have come to
> the union to talk about the problem and discuss what rights women
> have and how women can deal with the problem when they are
> battered. The husband of one of the members stopped battering his
> wife because he realized his violence would become known through-
> out the village. However, he was not able to control his emotions and
> thus cut off two of his fingers.

This case was presented by village participants Wang Hua Lian and
Li Sujin at the Negros Gathering for People's Alternatives, held in
the autumn of 1995.

The credit union strategy, which considers women's poverty and
lack of power as two sides of the same coin and seeks to solve both
problems simultaneously, has had remarkable success. Although this
is happening in small, remote, unknown villages in China, it holds
universal validity. When individual women come together to pool
their strength, it creates the power to change the existing situation.

> We wanted to expand this wonderful women's activity throughout
> Asia, and so we brought village women to Hong Kong and Negros
> here in order to develop a network of groups which have established
> alternatives in various parts of Asia. These women have seen the
> outside world for the first time and question the development policy
> that simply follows the NIEs. They showed strong interest in groups in
> other countries that are engaging in alternative activities. They learned

about examples of women's organization at the grassroots level in Asia, including Self-Employed Women's Association [SEWA] in India and the Grameen Bank in Bangladesh.

Lau sent three credit union members to the Alternative Farmers' Exchange Meeting held in Kerala State, South India, in March 1996.

> Let's extend and strengthen the women's network beyond national borders in order to create alternative development that differs from the current development model, which only increases the gap between rich and poor, and destroys the environment. To this end, the key is women's participation. To do so, we have to enact fundamental changes in the patriarchal structure. The Luxia and Wanli village example will serve as a good model of this alternative development

emphasized Lau at the Enoshima symposium. She concluded,

> The next challenge is how to connect these cases of micro-level alternatives, which are increasing throughout Asia, to create macro-level alternatives to change society and the development model.

How do we move from a point to a line, and from a line to fan out and cover the entire surface of Asia? This is related to the issue of how we overcome the strongly rooted free-market-economy development model that extends throughout Asia, and transform the industrialized countries' consumerism, which emphasizes only material prosperity.

Chapter 12

Weaving the Village Future: Thailand

A Village of Weaving Groups

After spending the night in a weaving village, in a rural home built high off the ground, I was awakened the next morning by village women's lively voices. They were already hard at work producing dye. In the yard, steam rose from two large iron pots in which tree bark had been boiling since the night before. The women were dipping skeins of white cotton thread into the pots again and again, after which they rinsed them in cold water. The pot of jackfruit-tree dye turned the cotton thread yellow and the pot of mango-tree bark dye turned the thread green. One woman pointed to a nearby tree on which the jackfruit had already grown larger than a baby's head, saying, "That's the tree that produces yellow dye."

Women were also gathered at a house several houses away, where they were dyeing cotton thread blue using the indigo plant boiled in pots lined up in the yard. One of each woman's hands was dyed blue by the indigo. Pointing to the dried plants tied together in bundles, which were leaned against the side of the house to dry, one woman said, "This is an indigo plant. It grows to this size in about three months." The women have learned how to create many colours using trees growing in their yards, plants raised in their gardens and wild grasses picked in the forests, engaging in a dyeing process that uses entirely natural substances.

We want to treasure the method handed down from our ancestors, especially since we have an abundance of natural materials here. Using chemical dyes would save labour but they are not good for health, as

Village women dye in many colours using traditional methods
and natural dyes

the steam rising from the pots of chemical dyes hurts our eyes and
noses. And when we dump the chemical dye, it pollutes the ponds
and the rivers, while the natural dye is good for the environment.

The women pointed out in detail the good points of natural dyes.
They all nodded in agreement, declaring, "Most important of all is
the beautiful colours of the natural dyes."

Almost every house in the village has a textile weaving loom.
Recently woven colourful cloth hangs here and there. In some
houses, grandmothers and daughters-in-law were happily engaged
in spinning thread together. The quiet village surrounded by the
verdant forest was overflowing with colour.

In Cokpukao village in Sakon Nakhon Province, located in northern Isan, a weaving project was started in the autumn of 1994. Moi, the leader of the project, a cheerful woman, the mother of two children, reported,

> All the women of Isan have traditionally been weavers. I was taught how to weave by my mother and I began to weave when I was 14 years old. I engaged in weaving to make my own clothes. When I heard that we could get some income if we formed a textile-weaving group and sold our products, I took a training course. Then, I suggested the possibility of forming a weaving group in our village. No matter how hard we work as farmers, our lives continue to be very difficult. I felt that we could use the period after the harvest, from February to July, more effectively in this way.

The weaving group, which began with thirty members, has doubled in size. The members discussed whether their weaving should be done using cotton or silk thread, and they decided to use cotton since it is essential for daily use. It could also be used for men's skirts, and it could be marketed locally. To set up the weaving project, they borrowed 30,000 bahts (US$750) from an NGO in order to buy cotton, which the members spun into thread, dyed and wove into cloth. The finished products are marketed through NGO networks.

The amount of income members earn depends on whether it is the busy farming season or not, but some months they can earn as much as 4,000 bahts (US$100) each.

> Most of us are burdened by loans borrowed at high interest rates from loan sharks or farmers' banks, because our husbands work as day labourers and earn only 50 or 60 bahts a day [US$1]. Therefore we will first use the money we make from weaving to clear up our debts. We also spend the money we earn on our children's education and on medical care.

Considering the average income of farmers in Isan, the income the women earn from weaving is quite high.

Women's Confidence and Men's Support

The women gain more from the weaving project than simply cash income. An elderly woman said, "After my sons went to Bangkok, I was lonely. But now, I am encouraged by our working together."

Village woman weaving cloth

"By receiving training in how to dye and weave, I have gained experience and knowledge, and have become confident", declared a young wife. Another woman said, "In the beginning, my husband did not seem happy about me going out to meetings, but recently he helps me to repair my weaving tools because he has learned that my work provides a good source of income." Thus, this weaving project has also changed the relationship between men and women.

Another positive result is that women do not have to leave the village to find work. "Although one of my friends invited me to go to Bangkok to work, I prefer to stay here and work with my family to working as a maid in Bangkok", said a 19-year-old woman. Moi related the weaving group's experience of trial and error, saying,

> The atmosphere of this village has become brighter. In the beginning, we produced only what was ordered. Because of our reputation for good design and high quality products, we received too many orders to have time for child-rearing and housework. We had to continue weaving until late at night using lamps, since our homes were without electricity. We thought the way things were going was not good, so we decided to sell our products through NGO channels.

She told me that a part of the profit was going into the group treasury, in order to achieve the members' dream of opening a shop in the village someday.

Women in Campon village in Roiet Province, in the southern part of Isan, where people were also conducting a weaving project, revealed similar feelings. Forty-six women from a hundred and thirty families in the village participated in the textile group, weaving silk for the most part. I was entranced by the sheen of the beautiful blue Thai silk cloth that was being woven, which Buala, 44, weaving group leader, showed me.

> The greatest advantage is the 18,000 bahts [US$450] annual income. But, in addition, I can also enlarge my vision by meeting people when I attend training courses, and gain skills in keeping accounts, management and records. Every day is happy because now we help one another in our village.

Buala had just been elected the chairperson of PANMAI, an organization composed of twenty-four village weaving groups in this province. "More than being pleased over being elected, I am concerned whether I can carry out my responsibility well or not. All I can do is do my best." This woman, who had never been out of her rural village before the weaving group was set up, has now assumed a heavy responsibility in the wider world. Witnessing this, I felt that Isan, the poorest area of Thailand, is certainly in a state of transition.

Establishing PANMAI

The word *panmai* means "many diverse trees" in the Thai language. PANMAI, which was set up in 1991, is a business enterprise comprising weaving group cooperatives in twenty-four villages, six regions, and three provinces in the southern part of Isan. PANMAI now has 500 members. The office of PANMAI stands alone behind a petrol station on the national highway in the Kasewisai District of Roiet Province. There, the cotton and silk cloth woven by village women is stacked high, and in a room lined with sewing machines, the cloth is made into dresses and blouses.

Poonsap Suanmuang, a PANMAI staff member who operates in the office very efficiently, is one of the organizers of the weaving project, having been engaged in the project for ten years. The Appropriate Technology Association (ATA) was founded in 1982 by scholars and engineers to spread grassroots techniques in order to achieve development in agricultural villages. ATA focused attention on traditional textile-weaving and established the Local Weaving Development Project (LWDP) in Isan. In 1985, Poonsap, who was then in her twenties and an LWDP volunteer, first went to nearby Sonhon village and started a weaving project to achieve women's self-reliance. The project has grown until, at present, twenty-four villages now participate in similar projects.

Rapid economic development in Thailand has taken place with the importation of modern technology; this has caused a breakdown in traditional village life. The weaving movement was a part of the appropriate technology movement which was founded in the 1970s by intellectuals who became concerned about this trend. Above all, it is noteworthy that this movement focused on women, who occupied positions on the periphery of poverty-stricken agricultural village society. Textile weaving became a key to reviving villages; integrated agriculture, which is spreading throughout Thailand, is also important – organic farming that produces rice, vegetables, fruit, fish cultivation and livestock without the use of chemicals for local consumption, rather than monoculture crop for export. "Our objective is not only to protect traditional village culture and increase women's income but also to empower women in agricultural villages, realizing that in releasing women's potential we will contribute to the self-reliance of entire villages", said Poonsap.

This weaving project has taken off with support from overseas NGOs including those in Japan, and LWDP initially took responsibility for marketing the products. Later, the women weavers decided they wanted to market their own products, and thus PANMAI was formed. Members contribute capital, purchase their products and market them through various NGOs, such as the Nature Shop, operated by women' groups in Bangkok. They even handle shipping products overseas.

Products bearing the PANMAI brand, including fabric, clothes, bags and accessories, are popular because of their natural colours unique to plant dyes, their dramatic prints and their original design. They represent the achievement of handmade beauty, and many Thai NGO women are fashionably attired in them. The 167 groups that stock PANMAI products pointed out as the top reasons for their choice "beautiful colours" (86 per cent), "made from natural dyes" (60 per cent), and "good design" (54 per cent). These results indicate that PANMAI brands are of good quality and fit consumers' needs.

"We came up with various ideas such as attaching labels to products to raise consumers' awareness that our products protect the environment, maintain traditional Isan culture and result in trade that benefits poor farmers", declares Poonsap, never forgetting her role as a consumer educator. Thus, PANMAI launched its marketing strategy; its profits totalled 150,000 bahts (US$3,700) and its gross sales exceeded 3 million bahts (US$74,000) in 1993. Using the profits as capital, PANMAI extended its activities and opened a petrol station in front of its office in 1995. The petrol station supplies low-cost fuel to the village. This is the first such attempt among NGOs and it is attracting much attention. Poonsap said, "The women members have gained confidence that women can engage in business." She supports members' plans to open a basic co-op or a rice mill in their village.

PANMAI also began to deal with the welfare issues of its members. "Since farmers are not covered by any social security, they have no support system in case of illness or death, not even to cover the cost of funerals. So we decided to start a life insurance and pension scheme." Under this system, 500 members pay 300 bahts (US$7) in annual insurance fees, which pay the family 100,000 bahts (US$2,500) in case of accidental death or 50,000 bahts (US$1,250) in case of death from illness. Under the pension scheme, members contribute 2 per cent of their profits and PANMAI also contributes 2 per cent.

PANMAI now anticipates that women members will become independent of the supporting NGO group LWDP and will be able to operate their various activities on their own by the end of 1997. Although the weaving movement has spread throughout Thailand, there are few projects as well organized as PANMAI.

Impressed by the activities of PANMAI, WAYANG, a media group that supports alternative development, produced an excellent documentary video entitled *Weaving for Alternatives!* and also published a book by the same name. These projects were produced to develop the Isan People's Handicraft Trade Network, founded as a result of the second international grassroots gathering, People's Plan for the 21st Century (PP-21), held in Thailand in 1992. The book and video call attention to women's efforts not only in Thailand but also in neighbouring countries such as Laos, Cambodia and Malaysia, which also have weaving traditions.

Women in Isan have quietly spun, dyed and woven cotton and silk cloth for many generations. The techniques and knowledge of village women that have been made obsolete by modernization have created an alternative development different from the destructive development that is attacking Asia. Travelling around to visit the weaving villages in Isan, I sensed the rich wisdom and overflowing power of impoverished women.

Women are the leading actors in the weaving movement, one of the farmers' movements to achieve self-reliance in Isan. At the same time, the movement for integrated agriculture, which enables the entire village to live in a more truly human way, is spreading. Since the 1960s, under the government agricultural policy to promote cultivation of agricultural products for export, Isan farmers have been forced to cut down the forest and to plant corn, tapioca and other cash crops in the vast area. This forced them to go into debt to purchase large-scale machinery, chemical fertilizers and pesticides. They became unable to repay these loans, due to the drop in the price of agricultural products on the world market.

Farmers began to implement an integrated agriculture, producing agricultural products for their own consumption, without destroying the environment. This includes digging ponds to cultivate fish, planting fruit orchards, restoring forests, cultivating rice and vegetables, and raising chickens and pigs. Women play a major role in this kind of agriculture as well. Women also bear major responsibility for village life when men leave home to work as migrant labour.

One More Challenge

On my way home from visiting the weaving villages, I stopped at Thanom village, on the outskirts of Surin city. There, four house-wives have been engaged in organic farming for the past two years,

> Once I went to the city to work. But I learned that I am not free if I'm employed by someone else. Now I can feel happy everyday while I am farming the fields here because I don't have to feel constrained by others. I get up at five o'clock every morning to gather vegetables, and my mother-in-law takes them to the market to sell. Just look at my fields!

declared Sanatai Somboon, 32, proudly. Many kinds of vegetables, including green onions, aubergines, garlic and hot peppers were thriving under the tropical sun in her garden.

"Once we get accustomed to chemical agriculture, we tend to fall into a vicious circle. The more we use chemicals, the greater the harvest. Some farmers even damage their own health. I came to doubt chemical agriculture and became interested in natural methods of agriculture." Sanatai, who exhibited an ability to take the initia-tive, found a farm family which was engaging in organic farming in another village and went to learn about it from them. Now, she produces fertilizer from chicken and water buffalo waste, and makes natural pesticides from the leaves of the nim trees that grow every-where in the area.

Walking on the footpath around a small fish pond, Sanatai spoke cheerfully, "We have rice, vegetables and fish here. I have never experienced a shortage of food. I sell vegetables in the market and earn 150 bahts [US$4] a day. I cannot imagine a better life than this." Linda Taraso, 33, who is also a member of the group formed by Sanatai, nodded in agreement, laughing as she said,

> Villagers often make fun of me, saying, "Why do you work so hard and get so sunburned? You'll never become a millionaire!" Although I may never be rich, I'll be happy if I just don't have any debts. My husband and I never fight about money.

Sanatai's husband has been to Taiwan to work and sent quite a large amount of money home, but he said, "It was not a place for human beings to work. I worked sixteen hours a day. It was hell!" Sanatai told me that, even now, some three hundred village people have gone to Taiwan to work; she felt concerned about them because of the news that their employer had been prosecuted by the authorities.

> Some husbands drink and are violent toward their wives. Some husbands go abroad to work and become infected with HIV there. Then they bring it home and infect their wives. We believe that women achieving self-reliance is one of the first steps in solving these problems. We will make every effort to increase the number of women engaging in natural farming.

Both Sanatai and Linda uttered the word *tamacha* (natural) again and again. These women believe that the self-reliance of women who care about the environment is the key to village self-reliance; they have taken the first step and are making slow but steady progress toward their goal. I sensed that they were also one of the sources of power for the construction of a new Isan, together with the women I had met in the weaving villages.

Chapter 13

The Wind of Change
in a Mountain Village: Nepal

International Women's Day in an Ancient Capital

The main streets of Kathmandu, the capital of Nepal, were filled
with more than one thousand women dressed in brightly coloured
saris on 8 March 1996, International Women's Day. Near the narrow
alleys of the ancient bazaar, Indra Choke, the area was so packed
with women that I was not even able to move. Women walked
along, waving red flags and raising their fists while chanting their
slogan, "Jindabad" (hurrah), over and over. The common theme of
this year's festivities was inheritance rights for women. The women
were attempting to change the system that discriminates against
them by denying girls the right of inheritance. Foreign tourists
looking into souvenir shops along both sides of the street were
surprised by the women's demonstration in the calm ancient city
that commands a view of the Himalayan mountains, and they stopped
to watch.

Mothers holding babies in their arms, sunburned old women
with white hair, all varieties of women participated in the demonstration. They came, travelling from distant mountain villages on
foot or riding several different buses, bringing with them the smell
of the soil from their home places. Urban activist women, their
saris fluttering in a stylish manner, and energetic women students
participated in the march, creating a lively atmosphere. Women from
around the world who had assembled for the 3rd People's Plan for
the 21st Century (PP-21) South Asia Conference also joined the
march, walking together with the Nepalese women.

Women marching in the demonstration in Kathmandu
on International Women's Day

I saw the faces of Khamla Bhasin, a leader of the women's liberation movement in India; Nimalka Fernando, from Sri Lanka, a leader of the Asian women's human rights movement; and Cecilia Rodriquez, of the Zapatistas, the organization of Mexican indigenous people that rose up for liberation. At the PP-21 conference Cecilia had spoken of her painful experience of gang rape at the hands of the Mexican military in Chiapas, the home base of the Zapatistas. She was deeply impressed by the grassroots women who rose up in this small Asian country of Nepal. In her speech, she emphasized the solidarity of women on the two continents, offering words of encouragement, and her words were greeted with hearty applause.

In Nepal, although since the 1960s a repressive one-party system called panchayat has dominated the government, of which the king is the central figure, the power of the people's movement has increased to the extent of establishing a multi-party democratic system in 1990. Since then, new women's groups have been formed one after another, and seventy-one groups were listed in the *Women's NGO*

Directory in 1994, of which forty-seven have been in existence since 1990. Including the women's groups affiliated to political parties, ninety-four groups joined together to found the Women's Security Pressure Group, having as its aim lobbying the government to expand policies on women.

> Women have played a very important role in the democracy movement. In order to realize the present democratic system, women have confronted the police all over the country, using their bodies as human shields. At least six women and one girl have been killed and hundreds of women have been arrested and tortured. Many women's husbands have been killed, leaving the women to struggle alone to raise their children. Because women have paid such a great sacrifice, it is meaningless for the new administration to establish a constitution that clearly states the people's sovereign rights unless discrimination against women is eradicated. Therefore, we continue to pressure the government

said Prativa Subedi, 41, who established the Women's Awareness Centre of Nepal (WACN) in 1991.

Village Women Speak Out

Prativa wrote the book *Nepali Women Rising*, appealing to women to have confidence. Believing that empowerment of women at grassroots level is most important, WACN is implementing a women's project to achieve self-reliance and, at the same time, constructing an advocacy campaign.

Twenty women from that village project came to participate in International Women's Day. Kabul village, which I visited with Prativa, was on top of a mountain more than one hour from Kathmandu by car and then one and a half hours on foot up a steep mountain road. "I chose this village as the site of the project after I learned when I taught here in my student days about the villagers' food shortage during the pre-harvest season from June to August and how much women suffer as they labour to draw water, having no wells." Although Prativa has an MA degree in economics and is an extremely intelligent woman, for more than ten years she has engaged in activities to support the rural women who compose over 90 per cent of all Nepalese women, in an attempt to liberate them from poverty.

Cheerful Maya Katoka (centre)

We waited for the village women to gather at the house of the village leader, located at the entrance of the village. It was a simple hut made of packed dirt. Inside, it was dark; the family kept goats in a dark area with a dirt floor, where children were moving around among the goats. There was almost no furniture, and the family lived a very humble life, indicated by the few clothes hanging on a wall. The yard commanded a splendid view of the Himalayas in the distance and the winding foothills in the foreground. I recalled the saying, "The Himalayas are beautiful, but the people are poor."

I saw many women wearing saris walking up the mountain in twos and threes. About twenty women sat in a circle on a mat spread in the yard. "I went to Kathmandu recently, where I shouted 'Equality between men and women!' It was such a great feeling! Returning to my village, I talked about it to everyone", said a cheerful elderly woman, Maya Katoka, 64. Her entire body attested to a lifetime of labour, including the deep wrinkles on her sunburned face and her strong, rough hands. "Because I do not own my own land, I work as a farm worker every day. Although men can earn 80 rupees per day [US$2], women get only 40 rupees. I used to accept this, but now I feel it's not right, it's unfair. So I went to Kathmandu to walk and raise my voice with many other women", declared Maya, her entire body revealing how she felt.

In this village, a women's group was formed, and five of the seventy-seven members participated in the International Women's Day March. This was a big adventure for women who were not allowed to leave their houses except to go to work in the fields and had almost never been out of their village. The stories the five women brought back from the International Women's Day meeting in Kathmandu made a big impact on the other village women. I heard that they had talked about nothing but International Women's Day for the last four days. When Maya said, "Before, we had to cover our mouths with a cloth whenever we spoke, but now we are free to speak out in public", the other women nodded in agreement.

Although these mothers spoke out cheerfully and frankly, each one had had sad and painful experiences because of their lives of poverty. Most of the mothers had lost several children: "I gave birth nine times, but only four of my children are still alive"; "Five of my eight children died." "I gave birth eleven times, but five of my children died. One child died six months after birth, another lived until the age of five. The saddest time was when I lost two children within a month", mourned a mother in her fifties, as she continued to wipe away her tears with her hand.

> I went to get water and I returned home to find that my child, who had a fever, had died. I had never been able to feed him until he was full. I was always so busy taking care of the house and working in the fields that I was not able to nurse him even after he became seriously ill. I couldn't even be by his side when he was dying. It happened a long time ago, but I still feel the pain whenever I remember. Every single time I lost a child, I became deeply sad. I always hid somewhere and cried alone. But I couldn't continue to cry; I had to feed my family. I could only find relief by working as hard as I could.

Although it has been somewhat alleviated, the infant mortality rate in Nepal still totals 139 out of every 1,000 boys and 145 out of every 1,000 girls under five years of age (World Population White Paper, 1996). Thus, Nepal has one of the highest infant mortality rates in Asia. Mothers who have experienced the loss of children are common in Nepal. "Recently, the number of children who die has decreased. Besides, we formed a women's group, so now we do not have to endure hardships alone. We can share our sadness and console one another and thus heal ourselves", said one village woman. "Even if someone is battered by her husband, recently, we have been bringing our problem to the group and work together to convince the husband to change. Because there are many cases in which husbands drink and abuse their wives, we are also dealing with the alcohol issue", said cheerful Maya.

The women's group that connects isolated individual village women crushed by poverty was finally organized three years ago after WACN members including Prativa made repeated visits to this mountain village. Prativa persisted in telling the village women, "Women cannot escape their subordinate lives until they can gain economic rights and receive education."

The members of this women's group divided into small groups to form a savings co-op into which each member contributes 25 or 50 rupees (US50¢ to US$1) per month to fund a project to raise chickens and goats, literacy classes, a well-drilling project, and a toilet-construction project. Women's activities like these have changed the very atmosphere of this mountain village. "When I visited this village as a student, it seemed like a dormant village. Now, it has become so vital that it makes me forget the weariness I feel in climbing up the mountain road", said Prativa.

The Village of Untouchables

The new wind blowing through Kabul village is also blowing through other villages throughout Nepal. This new force has been created by women. I visited two other villages where another women's NGO, Agriculture, Basic Health and Co-op (ABC Nepal), is located in a suburb of Kathmandu. Although the villages are not located in the mountains, I witnessed extreme poverty. I heard that poverty exists because many villagers belong to the lowest caste or Untouchable people, who have been discriminated against. In Dawnchi village, women have earned income by founding a co-op to raise goats and spin wool.

Amrita (left), leader of the women's group, is promoting
raising goats for a self-reliance project

"Because we do not own land, we went to work for a landlord.
We could only earn about 100 rupees a day, or 3,000 rupees [US$70]
per month by working twelve hours a day, beginning at four o'clock
in the morning. But now, through our co-op, we raise goats, and
earn about 6,000 rupees per month. The best thing is that now we
can send our children to school. Our life was very hard before, but
now I am happy", reported a woman dressed in a green sari. "I am
beginning to be able to afford kitchen utensils now, and my husband helps me. Our home has become bright", said a young mother,
holding her baby on her knee. The members of the co-op who

gathered at the village clinic said enthusiastically, "Our dream now is to open our own co-op shop."

I walked on a dusty footpath between the rice fields to nearby Kamital village. "When it rains, we cannot walk on this path because it is flooded", said Durga Girmire, the director of ABC, who accompanied me. There, I saw innocent-looking children playing, their faces and hands covered with mud and flies hovering above them. I learned that the village changed its name, which had meant "untouchable", three years ago. The village women supplemented their family's incomes by raising pigs and spinning wool.

Amrita Lishar, the leader of the women's group in this village, is a calm woman in her thirties who has three children and has suffered from her husband's violence. However, by participating in women's activities, she has regained her confidence. She began sending her two older daughters to school. Greeting her lovely daughters when they returned from school to a house as dark as a cave without anything like furniture, she said proudly, "They say that they want to be doctors when they grow up!" How much progress has been achieved when young girls who have had low self-esteem and an inferiority complex forced upon them are now able to verbalize their dreams for the future! Although the number of children who attend school has increased due to women's income-generating activities, girls continue to be considered inferior to boys. Therefore ABC is giving scholarships to ten girls, including Amrita's daughters.

The literacy rate in Nepal is quite low: for women over 15 years of age it is only 13 per cent, the lowest rate of any Asian country, meaning that 87 per cent of all Nepalese women are unable to read or write; for men over 15 years of age, it has reached 62 per cent, also the worst rate of any country in Asia (World Population White Paper, 1996). Although the literacy rate for school-age children is increasing, still only about 36 per cent of children aged 6 to 10 are enrolled in elementary school. The percentage of girls who enter elementary school in this age group is only half that of boys; furthermore, 77 per cent of all girls drop out of elementary school before graduation.

The reasons for this include the priority given to boys in circumstances of poverty – girls becoming busy with housework and care for siblings from about the age of 6, and the continuing tradition of child marriage in rural areas. According to the results of the 1990 survey "Girls' Labor Load: An Analysis of Poverty", among groups of children 6–9 years old and 10–14 years old, the labour load is heavier for girls than for boys, in both urban and rural areas. The rate of malnutrition among girls under 5 years of age is also double that of boys.

> The daughter is a thing to give away
> For someone else she is kept
> What a relief to send her away today
> I'm light as a feather and free from debt.

In her book, Prativa quoted this verse from a fourth-century play, expressing parents' feelings. This Hindu view of women remains deep-rooted even today, and girls are still looked down upon, regarded as less important and discriminated against in the home. As already mentioned, trafficking in young girls has not disappeared, because parents do not suffer a sense of guilt at selling daughters, who are regarded as worthless.

Change Begins with Children

> We conducted a rural development project focusing on care for children as the starting point, with very good results. Mothers gained confidence, enabling them to open a co-op shop last fall. I was invited to its opening and returned to the village for the first time in a long time. I was so happy to be there

said Sangeeta Shrestha, 35, a staff member of the South Asia chapter of the Norwegian NGO Redd Barna (Save the Children). This petite woman, dressed in a purple sari and smiling calmly, engaged in a unique agricultural development programme for four years, from 1989, called the Community Child Development Project in an area including six villages, with a total population of 24,000.

Lamjung district, said to be totally isolated, is a three-hour climb up a steep mountain road from the national highway between Kathmandu and Pokhara, a lake-side town. It commands a view of the snow-covered Annapurna mountain range. Sangeeta described how,

> We first approached neglected children in the midst of poverty and tradition. We adopted a strategy of assisting adults to change their lives, which will lead to the revitalization of the villages.

She frequently visited this district and endeavoured to organize the mothers, to enable them to start cooperative daycare, preschools and after-school centres for school-age children. She made special efforts to train leaders, and reported that,

> Although one woman named Jhuma was very afraid the first time she attended the training programme for the mothers' cooperative daycare programme, she became an outstanding leader within six months. Another woman named Durgamaya cried because of her husband's violence; however, other women pursuaded her husband to stop beating her, and now she, too, has become a leader and is doing her best.

Once they obtained confidence, the women began to work, starting literacy classes for mothers and girls, improving nutrition and addressing sanitary issues by building toilets. And ultimately they founded the Self-reliance Centre for Women. This also affected village men, who were influenced by the stories they heard at home from their children about what they had learned at the after-school centre. "Since village men also wanted to study, we started a class for fathers, dealing with child care, alcohol, violence and literacy. Now, men also have changed", said Sangeeta. Such a men's project is still unusual in Nepal.

Redd Barna published a book detailing the experience of Lamjung district, entitled *The Wind of Change*. "When I came to Lamjung, I doubted that we might be able to alleviate such malnutrition, such poor health conditions and such low status of women. However, this is an actual example showing that change is possible", said one of the workers at this project. Sangeeta said, "I think that women have the power to change Nepal!"

Chapter 14

Turning Pain into Power: Korea

The Continuing Pain of Torture

It was terrible torture! They said that I gave anti-government and subversive education to women at the Christian Academy. I was arrested for violation of the Anti-communism Law. I was brought to the headquarters of the KCIA [Korean Central Intelligence Agency], and was trampled on and beaten all over my body with a thick, square club by my interrogators to make me confess. I had black-and-blue marks, was bloodied all over my body and was no longer able to walk. I suffered so much I wanted to kill myself. The scars still remain.

At the Memorial Meeting to Remember the Kwangju Incident Victims, held in Tokyo in May 1996, Han Myung Suk, 52, who was studying in Japan, testified about her cruel experience in prison. She then spoke about the Kwangju Uprising. When citizens of Kwangju rose up in revolt against the dictatorial regime and were subsequently suppressed in a bloody riot that killed several hundred people, Han happened to be imprisoned in the Kwangju prison:

Suddenly I heard the sounds of repeated gunfire. A gun battle happened just beyond the wall of the women's jail, and at night I saw the flashes of gunfire. I had no way of knowing what was going on. I felt more dead than alive and I was trembling as I wrapped myself in the prison bedding.

Han, one of the leaders of the Korean women's liberation movement, doesn't appear to be a militant fighter, being a gentle woman. However, she has devoted half of her life to the agonizing struggle

Han Myung Suk told of her experiences in Tokyo

in Korea, which has seen the division of the Korean peninsula and a dictatorship that has lasted for thirty-two years.

Han participated in the opposition movement protesting the Korea–Japan Treaty when she was a student of Ewha Women's University. In 1968, she was arrested on suspicion of being a North Korean spy, together with her husband, Park Song Jung, who was a student of Seoul National University, just six months after their marriage, even though the charges against them were unfounded. Although Han was released on a suspended sentence, her husband was sentenced to fifteen years and was imprisoned in the Dae Jeon Prison. She was allowed to visit him only once a month. She continued both to encourage him during her monthly visits and to participate in the democratization movement. She also played an important role in the birth of the new women's movement.

> I first became aware of women's issues when I received adult education for women at the Christian Academy in 1973. I had never questioned women's traditional role, even though I had been involved in the student movement and the democratization movement. Therefore, learning about women's liberation for the first time was a shocking experience. The following year, I became an executive staff member of the academy, in charge of women's issues, and I became engaged in education to raise leaders for the new women's movement.

The graduates who studied adult education for women at the academy organized the Women's Social Research Group, which became the nucleus of the new women's movement. The group linked up with the women workers' movement that emerged in the late 1970s and worked to create a new feminist movement different from the conservative existing women's movement. Han explained:

> Under Japanese colonial rule, those pro-Japanese Korean women even collaborated in sending young women to serve as military sexual slaves, "comfort women", for the Japanese military. These women remained in leadership in the women's movement after the liberation from Japan at the end of the war and became supporters of Korea's postwar dictatorial regime. Such a conservative women's movement came under criticism in the 1970s. We continued the tradition of the Korean independence movement during Japan's Imperialist rule and now attempted to build a progressive women's movement that addressed both democratization and women's liberation.

The Women's Social Research Group of Han and her colleagues, together with the Ewha Women's University Korean Society and Women's Research Group, led the women's movement that emerged and gained momentum in the 1980s.

The Struggle of Women Workers

A driving force for the democratization movement and the women's liberation movement was the struggle of impoverished women workers. The starting point of their struggle was the immolation of a young man, Chun Tae Il, in 1970; he sought to achieve improvement in the horrendous conditions of women workers by sacrificing his life. The administration of President Park Chung Hee (1961–79), known as the Development Dictator, promoted an export-oriented high-economic-growth policy under the military dictatorship. There-fore Park's government was accused of working in collusion with Japanese business interests exploiting women workers, paying them extremely low wages. Indeed, it was the Korean version of the *Sad History of the Women Factory Workers*, a well-known Japanese book that documents the miserable conditions in textile factories during Japan's industrialization in the early twentieth century. Han reported:

> Women's working conditions were terrible at that time. Women were not treated as human beings; they were paid only 30 per cent of men's wages, were not allowed to go to the toilet freely, and were constantly forced to work overtime. All women workers became ill within five years. Learning of these wretched conditions, concerned intellectuals and students went into the factories to work for the purpose of raising consciousness and organizing the workers. I also worked in a wig factory for six months to support and organize the women workers.

Women workers did not patiently endure their situation. They struggled under the severe oppression of martial law, exerting a decisive influence on the democratization movement. In one case, in 1976, over 400 women workers at the Dong Il textile factory in Inchon opposed the company-affiliated trade union, and resisted the police by stripping to the waist, until they were taken to the police station. In another case, in 1979, over 200 women workers of the YH Trading Company opposed the closing of the factory and conducted a sit-in. One woman worker was killed and over a hun-dred women were wounded by police violence. These struggles of women workers will go down in history.

The Park regime strengthened its oppression, and in 1979, in the Christian Academy Incident, seven of the staff, including Han and another woman, were arrested. Han underwent cruel torture, as described in *Sekai*, a Japanese magazine of international affairs (Sep-tember 1979). She was sentenced to a two-and-a-half-year prison term, and put into the Saedaemoon (West Gate) prison in Seoul. It was rare for both husband and wife to be jailed as political prisoners. "On Christmas Eve, I happened to hear voices calling my name, 'Han Myung Suk, Han Myung Suk'. I learned that my friends had gathered outside the prison to encourage me. I was so strengthened by their voices!" However, Han was transferred to Kwangju Prison the following spring in order to separate her from her supporters.

Meanwhile, her husband did not even know that she had been arrested. He suffered when his wife suddenly stopped visiting him, thinking that she must have died in an accident or from illness. Six months later, his younger sister was finally allowed to visit him and, undetected, handed him a note when she shook hands with him. It was only then that he finally learned what had happened to his wife. "My husband was so pleased to know that I was in prison, because he thought that I was dead", laughed Han. The couple, detained in different prisons, were finally allowed to exchange letters once a month. "My husband gained strength during his time in prison by reading books and learning foreign languages; he was known as a bookworm. He even came to understand the theories of women's liberation better than I did."

Han was released from prison on 15 August 1981, after completing her two-and-a-half-year prison sentence. Her husband was released on Christmas Eve of the same year, after thirteen years' imprisonment. He was by then 41 years old, and she was 37. They started married life in poverty under the strict surveillance of the public security agency. After their release from prison, her husband began his study of Minjung (people's) theology in a theological seminary, and Han returned to graduate school at Ewha Women's University, quietly working to rebuild the women's movement.

Mothers' Protests

The dark 1980s, which opened with the Kwangju Uprising, was the decade in which the democratization movement reached its peak. Han escaped the eyes of the public security officials and founded the new women's organization, the Women's Equality and Friendship Association, in 1983. It was the first women's organization with a clearly defined theoretical framework and a sense of direction connecting women's liberation, democratization and reunification, and it worked for the protection of women's rights to survival, including those of women workers. Han was not able to serve as the visible leader of the new organization; thus, three young women, Iee Mikyung, Chi Eun Hee and Cho Hyoung, served as leaders. Today, all three women are at the forefront of the women's liberation movement in Korea in both practice and theory, as activists, politicians or academics.

However, the association underwent a split two years later, due to a difference of thinking within the group. Thus, Han began to concentrate her energies on support for laid-off woman workers, founding the Women's Democracy and Friendship Association in 1987, and enlarging the focus of her activities to include not only women factory workers but also women office workers, consumer co-ops and violence against women. Recalling that period, Han said,

> At that time, the democratization movement was at its peak, and women were playing an outstanding role. The Omoni [mothers] who had had their husbands, sons and daughters taken away led the anti-tear-gas struggle. Their cries directed at the police, shouting at the top of their voices, "Don't fire tear gas!", still ring in my ears. Citizens and students joined them in raising their voices so loudly that even the police flinched momentarily. Half of the people involved in such demonstrations were women. As a woman, I was very proud of their actions and I became quite confident regarding the strength of the Korean women's movement.

In the beginning, the mothers whose husbands, sons or daughters were killed, imprisoned for their participation in the democratization movement or committed suicide in protest became desperate or sank into despair. However, they became unyielding activists through their participation in the activities of the Association of Family Members of the Democratization Movement Activists. Twenty women wrote their touching experiences for the book, *Ah, Omoni, Your Tears: Memoirs of the Families of Korean Prisoners of Conscience* (1987), which was filled with the unforgettable *han* (deep sorrow and anger) of women in that period.

Amidst the rise of resistance against suppression in 1987, women in various fields came together to found the Korean Women's Associations United (KWAU), composed of over twenty women's organizations. Two women who were selected to serve as KWAU co-chairpersons were pioneers in the Korean democratization movement and the women's movement. Lee Oo Chung had led the Church Women United, had herself been arrested in the 1970s and had devoted herself to achieving the release of political prisoners. One of the symbols of the democratization movement, she was later elected a member of the National Assembly as a representative of the opposition party. Lee Hyo Jae was an internationally known professor of sociology at Ewha Women's University who was removed from her teaching position, but published the book The Korean Women's Movement during the Era of North–South Division. She actively engaged in academic research on family issues and also trained many women activist leaders. Both women represented the mainstream Korean women's movement.

One of the events that led to the establishment of KWAU was the Kwon In Sook sexual torture case in 1986, which brought the ongoing issue of sexual violence to public attention as a new problem to be addressed. The Korean Women's Hotline was established for the purpose of supporting survivors of rape and domestic violence, ten chapters were set up throughout the country; over 1,000 volunteers have been trained to engage in such activities. In 1993, the Special Law on Sexual Violence was passed, and protests about the sexual harassment case involving a professor at Seoul National University were carried out. Korean women also held a demonstration against sexual harassment, dressed in colourful chima chogori, the traditional Korean national dress, at the Beijing women's conference.

"Comfort Women" Break Their Silence

The sexual violence issue on which the Korean women's movement has focused in the 1990s is the military sexual slavery, or "comfort women" issue. It was Yun Jung Ok, former professor of Ewha Women's University's Department of English Literature, who created the opportunity for the harmoni (grandmothers), who were forced to become the sex slaves of the Japanese military and then keep silent for almost half a century after World War II, to raise their voices.

> During my Ewha Women's University student days, one day, we were called to a basement room and forced to put our thumbprints [equal to a signature in Korea] on a document. When I returned home that day, I talked about what had happened with my father. He became very anxious and made me quit university immediately. If I had not, I myself might have been taken as a member of the "Women's Volunteer Corps" [actually, military sex slaves]. Considering the agony experienced by many women my age, I felt that allowing that dark history to be forgotten was the same as killing them all over again.

Yun Jung Ok (right) with former North Korean "comfort woman"
in Pyong Yang

Yun's father was a pastor involved in the Korean people's independence movement, who refused to cooperate with Japan during World
War II. He hid his family at the foot of Mount Kumgang, where he
opened a private school. Yun returned to Ewha Women's University
after the war and later studied in England and the USA. Although
she enjoyed a successful academic career as an English literature
scholar, she decided to devote her later life to the "comfort women"
issue after retirement from the university.

Yun started investigating the issue in the 1980s, prior to her retirement. During a field trip to Japan in 1988, she travelled to Hok-
kaido, a northern island, and stood on the precipice of Cape
Tachimachi near Hakodate city. She learned that local newspapers
had reported during the war that many young Korean girls forced
to become "comfort women" had jumped off this precipice to commit suicide. She also visited Okinawa in the southern part of Japan
to talk with an elderly former "comfort woman" who was living out
a poor and isolated life. Then she flew to Thailand to talk with a
former "comfort woman" who had even forgotten her own language

and had survived only by clinging to her religion. She also visited Papua New Guinea to try to trace "comfort women" there.

She published a series of articles about this trip in the *Hangyore Newspaper* in January 1990. This stimulated the Korean women's movement to act. In May, the KWAU and other groups held a press conference, demanding a public apology and compensation for "comfort women" from the Japanese government on the occasion of President Noh Tae Woo's visit to Japan, for the first time, articulating Korean women's position on this issue both domestically and internationally.

In the autumn of that year, with the KWAU at the centre of the movement, thirty-seven women's organizations founded the Council for the Women Drafted for Military Sexual Slavery by Japan (Yun served as co-chair), which became the leading organization addressing the "comfort women" issue in Korea. Yun stressed repeatedly during her lectures in Japan that,

> The essence of the "comfort women" issue lies in the fact that the military of the Japanese Imperial Military Forces took young girls by force from colonized Korea, used them as a special gift from the emperor as a sexual outlet for Japanese military personnel and disposed of them afterward. This is a crime of the state which cannot be resolved unless the Japanese government pays compensation in recognition of state responsibility.

Following liberation, after the war, Yun, as the daughter of a father who had aspired to independence from Japan for the Korean people, had never once used the Japanese language, which had been forced upon the Korean people during the Japanese colonial rule of Korea. However, learning that some Japanese women were also seriously concerned about the comfort women" issue, when she visited Japan to conduct her survey in 1988, she decided that she would speak Japanese once again.

As a result of the campaign of women's organizations in Korea, in August 1991, for the first time, Kim Hak Soon came forward to reveal that she had been a "comfort woman". Since then, nearly 200 other *harmoni* have broken their silence. The House of Nanum (House of Sharing) was established in order to enable these women to live out the remainder of their lives in peace, for they had lived painful lives in isolation and poverty during the postwar era.

Then the women's movement strengthened its international

campaign, and former "comfort women" in various countries, including the Philippines, Taiwan, Malaysia, China, Indonesia and North Korea, came forward. The testimonies of former "comfort women" made a strong impact on the world at the World Conference on Human Rights in Vienna in 1993 and the Fourth UN World Conference on Women in Beijing in 1995, providing an opportunity for the international community to address seriously the issue of violence against women in wartime. Radhika Coomaraswamy, lawyer and UN Special Rapporteur on Violence against Women appointed by the UN Human Rights Commission, also researched the "comfort women" issue and produced a report recommending that Japan should pay compensation to survivors.

However, the Japanese government declared that, in the beginning, "it had been operated as a private business", and even denied any state involvement in the "comfort women" system. However, in 1992, after military documents had been unearthed, the Japanese government had to acknowledge the military's involvement in the system, but it has continued to adopt the official position that the compensation issue has been completely settled, based on bilateral treaties and agreements. In 1995, the Japanese government published a plan to establish the Asian Women's Fund as "one form of compensation" to which Japanese citizens are requested to contribute. This fund is strongly criticized by many of the former "comfort women" as "an excuse for the state to avoid assuming its legal responsibility".

> You can't restore the robbed lives and honour of victims by such a deceptive fund. Korea and Japan will never be able to establish a good relationship until the Japanese government assumes complete responsibility for the state's crime. We demand a solution of the "Comfort Women" issue for the sake of the future of both countries and peace in Asia,

emphasizes Yun, Despite her age, Yun continues travelling throughout the world bearing a vision of peace for Asia in the twenty-first century.

The Confucian Patriarchal System

Yun believes that there is one more aspect that must not be forgotten. She declares strongly,

The "comfort women" system constitutes gang rape institutionalized by the state. However, we must also recognize that it represents not only ethnic discrimination but also sexual discrimination. While the male perpetrators of rape can live out their lives with little concern for the past, the raped women were forced to endure even harsher conditions after the war.

From a woman's standpoint, Yun directs severe criticism not only at Japan but also at the Confucian patriarchal system in Korean society that forced these harmoni to remain silent for so long:

The "comfort women" issue is an issue that includes both ethnic problems and gender problems. While the men came back to their home country, many victimized women were not able to return home because of the shame they bore. Even if they came back, they had to live out their lives hiding from the public eye. The task of the women's movement is to eliminate this patriarchal system, this discrimination against women!

Han, who has engaged in research in Japan together with her husband since 1995, has been involved in a project to write the history of the Korean women's movement from the viewpoint of one of the activists involved, since she resigned as co-chair of KWAU in February 1996.

Since the 1970s, the Korean women's movement has moved forward, turning into strength the pain and the suffering of the poverty-stricken women workers and omoni who had their family members taken away during the democratization movement. In the 1980s, it carried on a campaign to integrate feminism and social change, in effect, democratization and reunification. Democratization has made progress since 1992, when Korea elected its first civilian president and two former military presidents, former-president Chun Doo Wan, who bears responsibility for the Kwangju Incident, and his successor, former president Noh Tae Woo, were arrested and stood trial.

In the midst of this increase in people power, the Korean women's movement is promoting women's political participation and working to achieve grassroots democracy. In the 1995 local elections, it campaigned for women to obtain 20 per cent of the assembly seats and succeeded in electing 128 women (5 per cent of the total). In the 1996 general election, Lee Mikyung, a co-chair of the KWAU, was among those elected.

"The sacrifice of so many people's blood and tears has brought us today's democratization. But the major issue of the reunification of North and South Korea still remains", declares Han. Believing that unifying the last separated nation remaining from the Cold War will serve to create peace in Asia, since 1991 Korean women have held four symposia under the theme Peace in Asia and Women's Role, in Tokyo, Seoul and Pyongyang. The several hundred Korean women who participated in the Beijing Fourth UN World Conference on Women and the NGO Forum demonstrated their great power through various activities during the conference.

The Korean women's movement has become a major social force as it faces new challenges, including philosophical confusion arising from the collapse of socialism and young women's decreasing interest in the women's movement due to the development of a consumer society. While basing its stand on nationalism, the women's movement is also seeking to move toward internationalization in this era of globalization. As citizens of a country in which rapid economic development has made it a leader of the NIEs, Korean women have begun to become aware of their responsibility for the damage Korea has caused other Asian countries as a result of its economic development. They declare, "Let us strengthen international solidarity with the global women's movement!" I anticipate the powerful role that Korean and Japanese women will play as they join together to create a peaceful East Asia in the twenty-first century.

Conclusion

Women Envision a New Asia for the Twenty-first Century

The Asian Miracle

It is said that "the twenty-first century belongs to Asia". Since the 1980s, the Newly Industrialized Economies (NIEs), such as Korea and Taiwan, have achieved rapid economic growth, followed by Southeast Asian countries. China has made a transition to a market economy, promoting economic development, followed by Vietnam. East Asia has become the "growth centre of the world" and the scale of these combined economies is about to exceed the economies of the USA or Japan.

"The Asian Miracle", "The Asian Era", "The Asian Challenge" and "Rising Asia" have replaced the "Stagnant Asia" of several centuries of colonial rule and its continuing legacy, to take its place on the stage of world history as "Growing Asia", within only two decades. It is estimated that the economic power of Asia, including that of Japan, will surpass that of Europe and the USA during the first part of the twenty-first century.

Indeed, whenever I travel within Asia I witness the extraordinary speed of economic development. When I visited Bangkok for the first time in the mid-1970s, I saw barefoot children wandering among food stalls and old Japanese taxis with their "vacant" signs still written in Japanese. It was such a poverty-stricken town. Today, there are said to be 1,400 high-rise buildings. The roads are packed with brand-new cars, causing constant traffic jams. The overwhelming affluence represents a very different world from both the Bangkok of twenty years ago and the rural Thailand of today.

When I lived in Beijing twenty years ago, it was a calm capital city, where clusters of bicycles and horse-drawn wagons passed along the wide roads. Today, however, highways run east to west and north to south, and high-rise buildings, including luxury hotels, line the streets, creating an imposing appearance. Men and women who formerly were clad in drab Mao style today wear whatever they like, brightening up the city with their colourful attire. From the main streets, it looks like a completely different city, and I can no longer walk about the city without a map.

How did such rapid economic development occur in Asia? Korea, which led the way for the NIEs known as the "Asian Tigers", has proceeded rapidly along the path of export-oriented industrialization under the direction of its government since the 1970s. The result has been the achievement of rapid economic development known as the Miracle of the Han river. In 1996, Korea joined the Organization of Economic Cooperation and Development (OECD) and has now become a member of the developed nations. Taiwan also adopted an export-oriented rapid industrialization policy by establishing export-processing zones earlier than other Asian countries. It is justly proud of its outstanding $10 billion (US$300 million) trade surplus, one of the largest in the world, and Taiwan's per-capita GNP now exceeds US$10,000.

Some Southeast Asian countries are already close to catching up with the NIEs. Among them, Malaysia received extended foreign capital from Japan and other countries by granting benefits under a Look East policy and constructed huge electronics industrial zones to provide products for the entire world. As a result, Malaysia has now achieved the highest per-capita GNP among ASEAN nations, with the exception of Singapore. The socialist countries, implementing such policies as China's Open Reform Policy and Vietnam's Doimoi New Deal Policy, have also transformed their economies into market economies competing for foreign capital, and have entered a period of rapid economic growth. The distinguishing feature of the Asian economic development policy is the market economy, promoted by states in cooperation with foreign loans and TNCs; in other words, industrialization and modernization achieved from above (states) and outside (foreign capital).

In the beginning, the USA extended economic aid to Korea and Taiwan, both of which had stood in the front line of the US anti-

Communist policy during the Cold War. Since the 1970s, however, Japan has become the prime source of economic funding, especially after Japanese business enterprises began to compete with one another in their advance into Asia, due to the influence of the strong yen resulting from the Plaza Agreement of 1985. Today, Japan's total investment in Asia and the Pacific Region has reached US93 billion, far exceeding the US investment of US$61 billion. In the case of Thailand, in 1988 alone Japan invested as much as its total amount of investment over the previous twenty years, due to Japan's Thai investment boom during the latter half of the 1980s. Today, some three thousand Japanese companies are operating in Thailand in various industries, leading to the criticism that "all of the forests, fields, and the seacoast of Thailand have been taken over by Japan".

Today, almost 40 per cent of Japan's trading partners are Asian countries, surpassing the USA and Europe and making Asia the most important market for Japan. In 1994, Japan's Official Development Assistance (ODA) reached US$13.2 billion, the largest amount of any nation in the world. Japan has consistently prioritized Asia, with China, Indonesia, India, the Philippines and Thailand being the top recipients of Japanese ODA; recently, China became the country receiving the largest amount of Japanese ODA. A massive amount of assistance in the form of yen loans is being poured into large-scale development projects geared toward industrialization. Thus, through its investment, trade and assistance, Japan is deeply involved in Asian economic development.

Development Dictatorship and Democratization

Asia's remarkable economic growth has been called "development dictatorship". We cannot ignore the reality that such remarkable economic development by military or dictatorial regimes employing violence and force has been achieved through cruel political oppression and human rights' violations. Behind the impressive GNP statistics run the blood and tears of countless persons. Korea suffered thirty-two years of military dictatorship from the time of the Park Chun Hee regime until 1992. Taiwan existed under conditions of martial law for thirty-eight years, under the Kuomintang (Chinese nationalist party) regime until 1987. Thailand underwent repeated military *coup d'état* revolutions. Singapore has continued its repressive rule under Prime Minister Lee Kwan Yu since 1965. Malaysian Prime Minister Mahatir exercises strong control under the Internal Security Act. Indonesia's military leader, President Suharto, continued his oppressive rule for thirty years, ever since the 1965 coup d'état in which it is reported that between half a million and a million people were slaughtered. President Marcos governed the Philippines from the same year, 1965, until his dictatorial government was toppled by people power in 1986.

Such economic growth-oriented development policy, which pays workers low wages and neglects the agricultural sector, is known as "Asian-style democracy", or "economic development over democracy". It results in strengthened militarization, a widening gap between rich and poor, environmental destruction, devastation of agriculture, dismantlement of local communities, and human rights violations. In other words, such a policy represents development achieved through violence: it is violence in the name of development.

People's revolts and struggles against such oppressive development systems in an effort to establish democracy have occurred repeatedly in each country. Bloody struggles such as the Kwangju Uprising in Korea in 1980 and the democracy movement in Thailand in 1992 delivered a shock to the entire world. As a result of similar sacrifices, a period of democracy has begun in Taiwan, Korea, Thailand and the Philippines. But just how many people have been murdered, imprisoned, tortured and executed in order to achieve this democracy? How many sacrifices have been forgotten in the darkness of history? And just how many people remain in prison? In walking through the prosperous streets of an Asian capital today, these victims come to mind. Can such cruel treatment ever be justified in the name of economic growth and development? How can Asia solve the dilemma between development and democracy, economic growth and democratization?

Women are the ones who suffered most under the economic growth achieved by the violence of the development dictatorship. The economic growth of Korea since the 1970s, based on export-oriented industrialization, was made possible by the exploitation of women workers.

> Even though Korea has achieved the Miracle of Han river, can we never fully compensate for the inhumane crimes committed against women factory workers? The cost will have to be paid. The Korea–

Japan relationship in this period is responsible for the anti-Japanese feelings of the Korean people that continue deep in Korean hearts!

says Chi Myong Kwan, who lived in exile in Japan for twenty years before returning to Korea. In his recent book, *Korea: The Road to Democracy*, he refers to the high economic growth achieved through the collusive Korea–Japan relationship.

The Impact of Globalization on Women

Some one hundred industrial processing zones geared to export products have been established in various parts of the world as hubs of the export-oriented industrialization policy. More than half are concentrated in East Asia and Southeast Asia. Attracted by promises of low wages and the "no taxes, no strikes" policy, TNCs involved in electronics, garment, shoe and toy manufacturing have advanced into these areas. Between 80 and 90 per cent of the workers in these factories are women. An NGO in Hong Kong summarized the result in a survey conducted in ten countries, entitled "Development for Whom?: Women in the Export Processing Zones in Asia" (1995), which describes the situations of these women factory workers.

> The average age of women workers is from 16 to 25 years, with the majority of them coming from agricultural villages. Their wages are low, around US$1 a day in Vietnam, China and Indonesia. They perform late-night work, and the ventilation and lighting are poor in their working environment. Occupational diseases, accidents and fires frequently occur. Their dormitories are crowded. They undergo sexual harassment and sexual violence both while commuting to work and on the work site. They are limited in the number of times they can take toilet breaks. Only single women are employed and those who marry must retire. Retirement is at a young age, and there is no maternity-leave system. Most factories prohibit the organizing of trade unions. Nevertheless, workers have engaged in strikes and protest actions, pressing for wage increases and improved working conditions in the Philippines, Indonesia, Malaysia, China and Korea. Some workers have been arrested.

In addition, TNCs operating in export-processing zones move their factories from one country to another freely, always searching for cheaper wages: from Taiwan and Korea to Southeast Asia, and from there to China and Vietnam, where wages are even cheaper. Purely economic rationalizations are at work here. The human rights of women workers who lose their means of livelihood as a result of factory closures are never even considered. One example is that of a Japanese company in Korea, Korea Sumida, which in 1989 informed women workers of the factory closure and dismissed them by sending a one-page fax. The struggle of the women workers of Korea Sumida, who went to the Sumida company headquarters in Japan to fight the company, represented the desperate resistance of women who will put their lives on the line to oppose such labour practices.

As the movement of capital has become more and more global, international labour migration has grown to an unprecedented extent, with tens of millions of people moving back and forth across national borders. The number of women who migrate from poor agricultural villages first to cities and then overseas has increased drastically. The feminization of international migrant labour has grown, and the sexual violence against overseas women migrant workers has attracted international attention.

Furthermore, the dramatic increase in the number of women seeking to make a living in the sex industry, both in their own countries and abroad, is also a product of globalization. Under the market-economy principle, everything can be sold, including the human body (blood, organs and reproductive ability); the natural environment, which has never been owned by anyone; education; information; scientific research; religion; the arts; and especially women's sexuality, being the "product" that reaps the greatest profit.

As mentioned in Chapter 1, the burgeoning traffic in women and children in Asia and other areas of the world is a modern form of slavery, not a business transaction carried out between equal parties. Those who are sold are people in a disadvantaged position, including poverty-stricken ethnic minorities, refugees, women and children, and those who profit by selling them occupy a strong position of power. Thus, the market principle produces competition accompanied by violence characterized by the survival of the fittest. Prior to the boom in the traffic of Thai women that started in the 1980s, Japanese men's sex tours in the 1970s were the object of international criticism. The Japanese sex industry, tied closely to criminal syndicates, has expanded dramatically, and a huge amount of violent pornography now invades our living rooms. This symbolizes the buying and selling of women's sexuality beyond national borders as a multinational-media sex industry conglomerate that has swept over Asia. This is the reality of globalization that violently exploits not only women's labour power, but women's sexuality as well.

Asia's rapid economic growth is also accompanied by violence against the natural environment. Large-scale development, including the construction of dams, highways, airports, seaports, industrial zones, plantations, shrimp cultivation and tourist resorts forces millions of people to move out of their homes, especially poor farmers, fisherfolk, urban squatters and ethnic minorities, even threatening their very right to survive. Environmental pollution resulting from industrialization is also worsening to a critical extent in every Asian country. During its period of rapid economic growth, Japan became a polluted island chain, as indicated by the Minamata incident, one of the worst mercury-poisoning cases in history. In Taiwan, as well, over forty rivers have died, cancer has become the leading cause of death, and there is grave concern about the devastation that will have been done to the environment by the year 2000. Major floods resulting from deforestation have claimed the lives of many people in Bangladesh, Thailand and Malaysia, and extraordinary droughts have caused starvation in many places throughout the world.

The women survivors of the Bhopal disaster in India, caused by an explosion at a factory producing agricultural chemicals for the US-affiliated TNC Union Carbide, and of the Chernobyl nuclear power plant disaster in the former Soviet Union, fought courageously because they realized that not only did these catastrophes rob their generation but also future generations of life. Violence against the natural environment has brought about mass violence reaching across generations and national borders, causing an unimaginable number of deaths. Therefore women are not merely the victims of environmental destruction; they have also become unyielding leaders of the environmental movement in every country. Reflecting this power, *Agenda 21*, adopted at the Environmental Summit in Brazil in 1992, devoted one entire chapter to stating the necessity of eliminating discrimination and violence against women and encouraging women's participation in policy-making in order to realize their further contribution to environmental protection.

Opposing Militarization

Asian women are also making a stand to oppose the violence of militarism and fundamentalism. In March 1996, PP-21 South Asia participants discussed their vision for the twenty-first century from the people's perspective, under the three headings of globalization, gender and alternatives. They considered gender – that is, how to change the social relationships between men and women – to be of critical importance. They focused on three points as major gender issues in Asia: globalization, militarization and fundamentalism.

The problem of militarization is that it accompanies the development dictatorship in East Asia and Southeast Asia, as in the case of the Philippines after the Marcos dictatorship was overthrown, when "total war" strategy against the anti-government opposition during the Aquino administration resulted in the murder of many people. Today, ethnic conflicts continue in Sri Lanka, Pakistan, Bangladesh and Burma, leading to the deaths of many people. Women suffer the losses of their families, are made refugees and are sacrificed through sexual violence such as rape.

Women are exposed to the danger of violence around the US military bases in Okinawa and Korea on a daily basis. For that very reason, women stand at the forefront of the anti-base struggle. The women's movement also confronted the issue of base prostitution even after the US bases were finally removed from the Philippines. It was women in Okinawa who played a key role in making the incident of the rape of a young Okinawan girl by three American military personnel an international issue. Seventy-one women, bearing the anger of this island of bases on which women had been raped and killed for fifty years, participated in the Beijing Fourth UN World Conference on Women and the NGO Forum. At one of their Beijing workshops, they made an appeal against the violent nature of military forces. Learning about this case of military gang rape of a 12-year-old schoolgirl (which occurred during the Beijing conference) only after they returned home, the Okinawan women held a press conference immediately to issue a protest. Their actions produced a wave that rocked the very foundation of the Japan–US security system.

Militarization has served to increase military expenditure, pushing women even further into poverty. After the end of the Cold War,

Okinawan women in Tokyo at the demonstration against US bases
in November 1995

Asian countries competed with one other in the importation of
weapons: Asia's share of weapons transactions reached almost 40
per cent of the world total from 1991 to 1994. It is estimated that
this percentage will rise even higher and that weapons imports to
Asia will exceed those to the Middle East, making Asia the largest
weapons market in the world. The top importers of weapons are
China, South Korea, Malaysia, Taiwan and Thailand, in that order.
The largest weapons exporter − in short, the major merchant of
death − is the United States. Today, Japan's military expenditure ranks
third, after those of the USA and Russia.

It is said that the ratio of defence spending to the total national
budget is especially high in Asian countries, and that the amount of
defence spending in southern Asia is double that of health and education expenditures combined. At PP-21 South Asia, Ritu Menon, a
feminist staff member of Kali for Women, an Indian women's alternative publisher, made the implications of this prioritization clear:

In Pakistan, US$27 per capita each year goes toward military expenditures, while only US$3 is used for welfare. Welfare spending per capita in India is US$9, and US$2 in Bangladesh. Although women have to walk for many hours to get water in both countries, India and Pakistan have the technology to deploy missiles in several minutes. Despite a serious food shortage, both countries use foreign exchanges to purchase weapons, spending five times as much to purchase weapons as that spent to purchase agricultural machines.

Militarization is a women's issue, she says:

Another reason why women participate so enthusiastically in the anti-militarization movement is not only violence against women and the sacrifice of welfare. An additional reason is that militarism is closely connected with masculinity; therefore, this is replicated in men's private lives as well, which serves further to strengthen military culture and patriarchal control.

Fundamentalism and Women

Muslim and Hindu fundamentalism are also major instigators of violence against women. Since the 1980s, South Asia has been shaken by ethnic conflicts based on religious fundamentalism. Recently, it has been reported that right-wing fundamentalism has become influential in shaping politics. Fundamentalism has strengthened the patriarchy and forced women either to become involved in armed conflict or to withdraw into the home. However, many women oppose this regression to tradition; thus, it was women's groups who first raised their voices in protest against the governments' Islamization policies in Pakistan and Bangladesh.

Islamic fundamentalism has also increased its strength in Southeast Asia, in such countries as Malaysia and Indonesia. This phenomenon is based on impoverished people's respect for traditional culture, based on their anti-Western, anti-US feelings. While 20 per cent of the world's poorest people receive only 0.5 per cent of the total income of the world, 20 per cent of the world's richest people control 79 per cent of the total income of the world. Poor people in Asia view this frightening North–South divide as coinciding with Western control of the non-Western world. In addition, this is also related to a dislike of the homogenized culture resulting from globalization. Male leaders in politics and religion who wield authority agitate this anti-Western feeling.

However, feminists in the Muslim and Hindu worlds which are experiencing the rise of fundamentalism have asserted that violence should not be tolerated in the name of traditional religion and culture. They have moved to eliminate violence and discrimination caused by traditional patriarchal customs such as female infanticide, female genital mutilation, dowry murder, suti (wives being cremated along with their deceased husbands' remains), temple prostitution, punishing women by flogging or stoning, and denying women the right of inheritance. Furthermore, women are seeking their rights to self-determination on issues of sexuality that have not been permitted by conservative religious authorities, including the Catholic Church, throughout the world, and have continued the campaign for the global acknowledgement of women's reproductive and sexual rights.

Accompanying the rise of the women's movement, in 1993 the World Conference on Human Rights in Vienna clearly defined "women's human rights", and the UN, building on this, approved the "Declaration on the Elimination of Violence against Women" at the end of the same year. This declaration characterizes domestic violence and violence deep-rooted in tradition, long regarded as personal and private issues, as human rights violations. Reproductive rights were recognized as a basic human right of women at the Population and Development Conference in Cairo in 1994, and the Platform for Action of the Beijing World Conference incorporated the issue of sexual rights in a substantial way. The twentieth century will be remembered as the century in which the women's liberation movement and feminism shaped world history.

However, the conservative powers in Asia that assert the need for the protection of culture and tradition against Western values are rejecting the concepts of human rights and democracy. Against the West's emphasis on the universality of human rights, China emphasizes the state's sovereignty; Malaysia and Indonesia place priority on economic development; and most Islamic countries advocate cultural relativism. Thus, the governments of Asian countries are advocating Asian values and strengthening criticism of the West. On the other hand, however, the governments of every country in Asia are promoting economic development via the market economy system based on the modern Western model. During the Meiji era, Japan espoused the slogan "Japanese Spirit and Western Technology".

It adopted Western scientific technology and industrialization, while hesitating to accept Western values such as democracy and human rights in order to maintain Japan's feudal tradition, which led to militarism. Today, Asia is running at full speed on a similar path advocating an "Asian Spirit and Western Technology" development policy. But even if Asia continues in the same direction and overtakes the West as an economic power in the twenty-first century, the question remains: can Asia inherit and further develop democracy and human rights, developed in the West, to create new human values and alternative cultures that surpass those of the West?

Three Forms of Modern Western Violence

Asian feminists have already launched various activities in search of an alternative society. One of the first signs of this movement was Development Alternative for Women in a New Era (DAWN), created by women of the South, which was born at the Nairobi World Conference on Women. DAWN has spread to three continents and was visibly active at the Beijing conference, demonstrating its influence:

> In the 1970s, the United Nations' Women Decade attempted to integrate women into development. However, the situation of women only worsened. Therefore, since 1980, the year of the World Conference on Women in Copenhagen, there has been recognition of the necessity to change the very model of development, and with this began discussions of alternative development. DAWN researched and conducted surveys on the impact of economics on women, and issued proposals at UN conferences and other international forums. Finally, our ideas have been adopted due to the growing strength of the international women's movement in the 1990s

said Peggy Antrobus, DAWN's present coordinator, from Barbados. DAWN pursues "humane and sustainable development through the empowerment of women". At the Beijing conference Antrobus pointed out the following three strategies to achieve this goal: (1) pressing the World Bank and TNCs to take responsibility for globalization; (2) changing states to become more democratic and transparent; and (3) strengthening civil societies domestically and internationally.

ISIS Manila International, an international women's media network with headquarters in Manila, published Remaking the Economy in 1995, containing ten theses and reports, mainly by Asian women. It pointed out that "in the last few years, feminist scholars and researchers, as well as advocates and grassroots women, have engaged in debate about the dominant economic framework. They have called for the creation of a new economic framework that incorporates economic prosperity and women's emancipation." Based on the perspective of women, they seek to change male-invented economics.

The current global market economy — that is, the free-trade movement — is a policy promoted by men that places priority on growth. It has widened the gap between North and South, rich and poor, and has caused environmental destruction. In addition, it strengthens the subordination of women because it emphasizes the production of goods to the neglect of reproduction and care for human life; therefore women require an alternative economic system. An economics that has been challenged from the viewpoint of environment and ecology is now under pressure from the gender and feminist perspective.

On the eve of the twenty-first century, the crisis of poverty, violence and environmental destruction is worsening, against which Asian ecological feminists are issuing a basic challenge. Japanese mainstream feminism is critical of ecology, which tends to glorify motherhood, while other Asian feminists are strengthening feminist women's consciousness in their desperate struggle for survival against environmental destruction. For them, ecology and feminism are one.

Vandana Shiva, an Indian physicist and leading advocate of this thinking, has become a strong critic challenging modern Western technological civilization as a result of her involvement in the grass-roots women's struggle, such as the Chipco movement, in which Himalayan village women protected their forests by hugging the trees. Her first book, published in 1988, *Staying Alive: Women, Ecology and Development*, states,

> With the destruction of forests, water and land, we are losing our life-support systems. This destruction is taking place in the name of "development" and progress, but there must be something wrong with a concept of progress that threatens survival itself. The violence against nature, which seems intrinsic to the dominant development model, is also associated with violence against women who depend on nature for drawing sustenance for themselves. This violence against nature and women is built into the very mode of perceiving both, and forms the basis of the current development paradigm.

Thus Shiva exposes the basis of the domination of the South by the North.

The five hundred years of Western modernization since Columbus could not have been realized without colonial domination, the conquering of nature and patriarchy; in other words, it has been realized through violence perpetrated against the South, against the natural environment and against women. The root cause of the ecological crisis can be seen to be the obliteration of the feminine principle: living in harmony with nature and supporting life.

Reclaiming Feminine Values and the Empowerment of Women

It was Kamla Bhasin, an Indian feminist, who first labelled development that leads to violence, destruction and death as "male development". Bhasin delivered the keynote address at the PP-21 South Asia main forum, held in Kathmandu, Nepal, on International Women's Day, 8 March 1996. In her speech, she rejected the current development model and issued a strong appeal for the restoration of democracy and feminine values, stating:

> Let us strengthen democracy at all levels. If we have participatory democracy, no outsiders can come and plunder our forests or seas, flood our markets with non-essential goods; no government and no bank can make dangerous dams against the wishes of local communities; no dictator can stifle the voices and choices of people in Burma; the USA cannot have military bases in the Philippines; no nuclear testing can be done in the Pacific Islands; no dangerous wastes from the so-called developed countries can be dumped in the Third World; no one can turn our children into child labour; no religious and political leaders can create religious and other wars.
>
> The struggle for democracy is also a struggle for a better economic order.... For us women, the struggle for democracy is also the struggle for women's dignity. The other side of the Vietnam War was the brothels set up in Bangkok and Manila. The war is over but the war against women continues. It is the economic warriors from Japan and Germany who frequent these brothels.
>
> True democracy and human rights have also to be respected within the family. Women are battered and raped within the family; they are forced into prostitution....
>
> Let us nurture the woman in us. Women can play a special role to halt the process of destruction and the violence. Feminine values

Kamla Bhasin (second from right) appeals for human rights at the demonstration of Women in Black at the NGO Forum in Beijing

contain the key to our survival. What is feminine? Nurturing, caring, being like nature, non-violent, and non-specialized have been labelled feminine and therefore looked down upon, marginalized or crushed. Killing of the feminine is what has made our world today so inhuman. The feminine or human values are found more easily in women than in men, not because of the female body, but because of historical and sociological reasons.

The biggest threat to the twenty-first century is violence. The hope comes from the fact that these struggles are converging. There is globalization of people's struggles. There is multinational cooperation. People are creating alternatives.

Disavowing the negative aspects of the Western modernization of developmentalism, deepening and enriching democratic and human rights principles inherited from the West, as the basis for the liberation of oppressed peoples, Bhasin seeks to create a society in which feminine values are universalized. She envisions the creation of a new Asia, built on the trinity of feminism, ecology and democracy. This powerful vision for the future, which Asian women have worked out in their resistance to "mal", "male-centred" development, is most convincing and is attracting widespread attention. This vision also represents a search for a truly Asian feminism.

What women are aiming at is not an Asia that has undergone development and destruction created on male principles such as domination, competition, efficiency, plundering and homogenization, but an Asia characterized by symbiosis and human rights based on feminine principles such as self-reliance, solidarity, caring, sharing and diversity. In order to achieve this Asia, we must make basic changes in corporate-controlled and male-dominated society, and instead create a society in which both men and women can live more fully human lives.

Looking back over the twentieth century, we find that more human lives have been lost in this century than in any previous century, due to war, dictatorship, starvation and environmental disasters. Now this century of genocide is approaching its end, and a new century and millennium are about to begin. As a woman living at such a significant time in history, I strongly desire to participate in the creation of a twenty-first century totally different from the twentieth century.

The key to this is the empowerment of women. But by empower, what kind of power do we mean? Not the power to dominate, invade, conquer, exploit, control, impose authority. It is the power to think independently and make our own decisions; the power that instils confidence and pride in being a woman; the power to determine our own life course; the power to share pain with those discriminated against and oppressed; the power to value the natural environment and human life; the power to act against oppression and destruction and for social change; and the power to create a new culture and new values.

If the women who are filled with such power increase and unite, they can move forward in history, overcoming the monstrous global force. I would like to take the first step toward the twenty-first century, joining together with other empowered Asian women.

Index

Page numbers in *italics* refer to illustrations.

Books of Related Interest from Zed

Women in Asia

Women's Asia
Yayori Matsui

Capital Accumulation and Women's Labour in Asian Economies
Peter Custers

Embodied Violence: Communalising Female Sexuality
in South Asia
Edited by Kumari Jayawardena and Malathi de Alwis

Of Woman Caste: The Experience of Gender in Rural India
Anjali Bagwe

Frogs in a Well: Indian Women in Purdah
Patricia Jeffery

Gender and Tribe: Women, Land and Forests
Govind Kelkar and Dev Nathan

Purity and Communal Boundaries:
Women and Social Change in a Bangladeshi Village
Santi Rozario

Where Women are Leaders: The SEWA Movement in India
Kalima Rose

Women and Right-Wing Movements: Indian Experiences
Edited by Tanika Sarkar and Urvashi Butalia

Gender and Slum Culture in Urban Asia
Susanne Thorbek

Arguing with the Crocodile: Gender and Class in Bangladesh
Sarah White

Changing Identites of Chinese Women: Rhetoric, Experience and
Self-Perception in Twentieth-Century China
Elisabeth Croll

Women and Chinese Patriarchy: Submission, Servitude and Escape
Edited by Maria Jaschok and Suzanne Miers

International Women's Movements

A Diplomacy of the Oppressed:
New Directions in International Feminism
Edited by Georgina Ashworth

Subversive Women: Women's Movements in Africa,
Asia, Latin America and the Caribbean
Edited by Saskia Wieringa

Women and Empowerment: Participation and Decision-making
WOMEN AND WORLD DEVELOPMENT SERIES
Prepared by Marilee Karl

Women and Violence

States of Conflict: Gender, Violence and Resistance
Edited by Susie Jacobs, Ruth Jacobson and Jennifer Marchbank

Gender and Catastrophe
Edited by Ronit Lentin

What Women Do in Wartime: Gender and Conflict in Africa
Edited by Meredeth Turshen and Clotilde Twagiramariya

Women and Violence: Realities and Responses Worldwide
Edited by Miranda Davies

Women and War
Jeanne Vickers

The Blue Room: Trauma and Testimony Among Refugee Women
Inger Agger

Gender and Economics

Women, Population and Global Crisis:
A Political-Economic Analysis
Asoka Bandarage

The Strategic Silence: Gender and Economic Policy
Edited by Isabella Bakker

Paying the Price: Women and the Politics of
International Economic Strategy
Mariarosa Dalla Costa and Giovanna F. Dalla Costa

Patriarchy and Accumulation on a World Scale:
Women in the International Division of Labour   NEW EDITION
Maria Mies

Women and the New World Economy
Gita Sen

Mortgaging Women's Lives:
Feminist Critiques of Structural Adjustment
Edited by Pamela Sparr

Women and the World Economic Crisis
WOMEN AND WORLD DEVELOPMENT SERIES
Prepared by Jeanne Vickers

Women, the Environment and Development

The Women, Gender and Development Reader
Edited by Nalini Visvanathan with Lynn Duggan, Laurie Nisonoff and Nan Wiegersma

Staying Alive: Women, Ecology and Development
Vandana Shiva

The Daughters of Development:
Women in a Changing Environment
Sinith Sittirak

Women, the Environment and Sustainable Development:
Towards a Theoretical Synthesis
Rosi Braidotti, Ewa Charkiewicz, Sabine Häusler and Saskia Wieringa

Getting Institutions Right for Women in Development
Edited by Anne-Marie Goetz

Feminist Perspectives on Sustainable Development
Edited by Wendy Harcourt

The Elusive Agenda: Mainstreaming Women in Development
Rounaq Jahan

Making Women Matter: The Role of the United Nations
Hilkka Pietila and Jeanne Vickers

Ecofeminism
Maria Mies and Vandana Shiva

Gender, Education and Development
Edited by Christine Heward and Sheila Bunwaree

Third World Second Sex
Edited by Miranda Davies

The Power to Change:
Women in the Third World Redefine their Environment
Women's Feature Service

African Women and Development: A History
Margaret M Snyder and Mary Tadesse

Gender and Development in the Arab World:
Women's Economic Participation – Patterns and ~~ie~~
Edited by Nabil F. Khoury and Valentine M. Moghadam

Biopolitics: A Feminist and Ecological Reader
Edited by Vandana Shiva and Ingunn Moser

Women and the Environment
WOMEN AND WORLD DEVELOPMENT SERIES
Prepared by Annabel Rodda

Women's Rights as Human Rights

Refugee Women
WOMEN AND WORLD DEVELOPMENT SERIES
Prepared by Susan Forbes Martin

The Trade in Domestic Workers:
Causes, Mechanisms and Consequences of Internation~~al~~ ~~on~~
Edited by Noeleen Heyzer, Geertje Lycklama à Nijeholt and Nedra ~~~~

Ours by Right: Women's Rights as Human Rights
Edited by Joanna Kerr

The Circumcision of Women: A Strategy for Eradicatio~~n~~
Olayinka Koso-Thomas

A World of Widows
Margaret Owen

Injustice Systems: Women's Access to the Law
Edited by Margaret Owen and Georgina Ashworth

The Traffic in Women:
Human Realities of the International Sex Trade
Siriporn Skrobanek, Nataya Boonpakdee and Chutima Jantateero

Women and Human Rights
WOMEN AND WORLD DEVELOPMENT SERIES
Prepared by Katarina Tomasevski

These books should be available from all good bookshops.
In case of difficulty, please contact us:

Zed Books Ltd, 7 Cynthia St, London N1 9JF, UK.
Tel +44 (0)171 837 4014; Fax +44 (0)171 833 3960
e-mail: sales@zedbooks.demon.co.uk